Jan 2004

Jan 2004

SOFT
FURNISHINGS
WITH CALICO
RIBBON AND LACE

SOFT FURNISHINGS WITH CALICO
RIBBON AND LACE

FIONA REEVES

PHOTOGRAPHY BY ANTHONY JOHNSON
ILLUSTRATIONS BY ALIX GRACIE

Published in the UK in 1995 by
New Holland (Publishers) Ltd
24 Nutford Place
London W1H 6DQ

Copyright © in text Fiona Reeves 1995
Copyright © in photographs Struik Image Library: Photographer Anthony Johnson 1995
Copyright © in illustrations Struik Image Library: Illustrator Alix Gracie 1995
Copyright © in printed edition New Holland (Publishers) Ltd 1995

EDITORS Laura Milton and Elizabeth Frost
DESIGN Petal Palmer
COVER DESIGN Petal Palmer
PHOTOGRAPHY Anthony Johnson
PHOTOGRAPHIC STYLING Vo Pollard
ILLUSTRATIONS Alix Gracie
DESIGN ASSISTANT Lellyn Creamer

Typesetting by Darryl Edwardes
Reproduction by Hirt & Carter (Pty) Ltd
Printed and bound by Tien Wah Press (Pte.) Ltd, Singapore

ISBN 1 85368 336 1

ACKNOWLEDGEMENTS
My first thank you goes to Linda de Villiers for having faith in me; then, to my mom, dad, Charlene and
Lauretta and all my dearest and close friends, for motivating and encouraging me to finish this book, and to
my children, Jethro and Cleo, because without them I would never have started my business.
My thanks also to my assistant, Romé Carstens, for all her help and patience during the last few hectic
months of producing this book; to Petal Palmer, Laura Milton and Elizabeth Frost for making me feel very
special and for their encouragement, and to Anthony Johnson for the beautiful photographs.
A special thank you also goes to Vo Pollard for her friendship, guidance and empathy during the many
long and hard hours spent on photographic styling.

CREDITS
The publishers extend their thanks to Maud Louw, Martha's Vineyard, Stuttafords Ltd.,
Block & Chisel, Bric-à-Brac Lane and China Rose for the loan of props for photography, and to
Auberge Penrose and Annatjie Opperman for providing a location for some of the photographs.

CONTENTS

INTRODUCTION 7

GENERAL TECHNIQUES 8

THIS BOOK IS DEDICATED
TO MY MOTHER.

INTRODUCTION

Although I grew up in a family where my mother and sisters were able to sew, it was only after I had completed my schooling, enjoyed an exciting career and started my own family that my interest in needlework began.

I settled down to motherhood quite happily, but after a few months I realized that I needed to occupy myself with something more stimulating than nappies and baby bottles. My mother suggested that I make a few scatter cushions for the local craft market, and much to my surprise, they all sold! Motivated by this and loads of encouragement from my family, I started making other items. My home industry had begun.

Today, after six years, I run my own successful home industry and have built up a reputation for good quality country decor that has its own distinctive style.

CALICO, THE NATURAL ALTERNATIVE

The fabric that I have used to make the articles featured in this book is an organic vegetable cloth commonly known as *calico* or *seedcloth*. Good quality calico is 100 per cent cotton, unbleached and fully washable, and should also be preshrunk.

As it has a neutral colour, calico is extremely versatile, and can be used to create a number of different 'looks'. Combined with lace and ribbon, it can be pretty and cottagey; with contrasting piping, simple yet elegant.

Calico can also provide the ideal solution to a decor problem. If, for example, you are stuck with a busy carpet or wallpaper that will be too expensive to replace, or if the room is very dark and needs brightening up, calico curtains or accessories will do the trick. Calico can be used as curtaining throughout the house, but with a little imagination and by using contrasting valances or tiebacks in various colours or patterns, every room can be made to look quite different. The colour scheme can later be revamped by simply changing the tiebacks or valances. Should you wish to replace the curtains at some stage, extend their life by using them as linings.

This book contains fully illustrated, detailed, step-by-step instructions for making a variety of useful small items such as a lingerie bag, a tissue box cover, a fabric mirror surround and a lampshade. It also shows you how to approach a selection of more complicated projects such as scatter cushions, regular and Continental pillowcases, duvet covers and night frills, and a unique comforter, and includes guidelines on how to measure and make curtains, valances, tiebacks and blinds.

In keeping with my philosophy that everything should be pretty but practical, each item is made in such a way that it can be removed if necessary, and washed with the minimum of fuss. I am confident that you will soon find, as I have, that with the minimum of cost and effort, calico can be used to transform any room – with highly effective results.

Fiona Reeves

GENERAL TECHNIQUES

NOTE The seam allowance for all projects is 1 cm (⅜ in), unless otherwise stated. To reduce bulkiness, trim the seam to 5 mm (¼ in) where necessary.

MAKING A FRENCH SEAM

A French seam is a neat, strong seam, stitched once on the right side and once on the wrong side, that is very useful for seams that will be visible, or those on items that will be laundered frequently.

With the wrong sides of the fabric together, stitch a narrow, 5 mm (¼ in) seam; press seam open. Now, with right sides together, stitch a slightly wider seam, enclosing the first seam in the process (see Figure 1). Press.

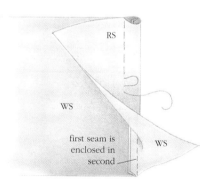

first seam is enclosed in second
RS
WS
WS

FIGURE 1

As an alternative to making a French seam, simply stitch the two pieces of fabric together, with right sides together, leaving a 1 cm (⅜ in) seam allowance. Overlock or zigzag the raw edges together to finish off and press the seam allowance to one side.

GATHERING A FRILL

A frill can be gathered in different ways; your choice depends on the attachments and stitches offered by your sewing machine or overlocker.

If you are gathering a fairly long piece of fabric, follow this basic procedure, regardless of which gathering method you are using: divide the raw edge of the fabric for the frill and the edge of the item to which the frill will be attached into four or six equal sections and mark with pins. Using one of the methods suggested below, gather the frill so that each section will fit the relevant section on the item. (It may be best to gather each section separately, to avoid having long, continuous pieces of thread, which may break when gathered.) With right sides together, pin and then stitch the gathered edge of the frill to the edge of the item. Trim and neaten the raw edges if necessary.

❋ Use the ruffle foot attachment on your machine to gather your frill to the required length.

❋ Set the zigzag stitch on your sewing machine at its widest, and, working on the wrong side, zigzag over a length of crochet thread, taking care not to catch the thread in the stitching (see Figure 2a). Gently pull the crochet thread to gather the frill.

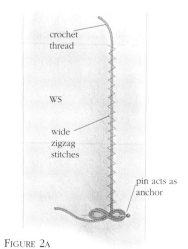

crochet thread
WS
wide zigzag stitches
pin acts as anchor

FIGURE 2A

❋ Having loosened its top tension slightly, set your sewing machine on the longest stitch. Working on the right side of the fabric to be gathered, stitch two parallel rows of straight stitches about 5 mm (¼ in) apart, leaving long threads loose at each end. Stop stitching when you reach a seam, starting again on the other side, as it is difficult to gather through two thicknesses. Anchor your threads with a pin at one end, and gently pull from the other, while pushing the fabric along the threads to create even gathers. Anchor at the other end once you have achieved the desired length (see Figure 2b).

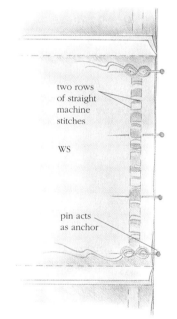

two rows of straight machine stitches
WS
pin acts as anchor

FIGURE 2B

To attach a frill around the edges of a cushion cover, for example, pin into position, with right sides and raw edges together, along the gathered edge of the frill. Stitch the frill down carefully, taking care to round the corners slightly. Swing your work round and tuck the frill back as you go to avoid catching it in the line of stitching. Stitch the two loose ends of the frill together using a French Seam (see Making a French seam, this page) and stitch the remaining section of the frill into place.

JOINING RIBBON AND LACE

Pin the ribbon or lace into position, leaving an extra 2 cm (¾ in) loose at one end. Stitch the ribbon or lace down using one or two rows of straight stitches. At the end, make a neat join, folding the longer end over and stitching it down securely over the other end (*see* Figure 3). Do not position this join exactly over other joins or seams, as it becomes rather bulky.

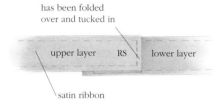

has been folded
over and tucked in

upper layer   RS   lower layer

satin ribbon

FIGURE 3

MAKING PIN TUCKS

Pin tucks add a simple but effective decorative finish to cushions, pillowcases, tablecloths, and so on. They vary in size, ranging from a depth of a few millimetres to about 1 cm (⅛–⅜ in) – I usually make mine about 3 mm (⅛ in) deep. Allow extra fabric for pin tucks when planning your project – simply multiply the number of pin tucks by twice the finished size of each one.

Working on the right side of the fabric, mark the position of the centre pin tuck, fold along this line, and press. Neatly stitch your pin tuck into position using a line of straight stitches 3 mm (⅛ in) – or whatever size you'd like your pin tucks to be – from the fold.

Open out your fabric and mark the positions of the pin tucks on either side of the centre pin tuck, making sure that they are equal distances from the centre. Once your pin tucks are complete, press so that they all lie in the same direction (*see* Figure 4).

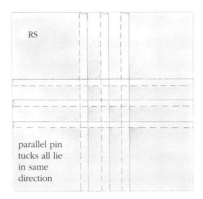

RS

parallel pin
tucks all lie
in same
direction

FIGURE 4

INSERTING LACE

Give an item a pretty, delicate look by inserting lace between sections of fabric – a simple but very effective procedure.

Once your project is almost complete (if, for example, you are making a lampshade, complete the casings and join the two short sides of the rectangle to make a tube first), make two soft pencil lines in the appropriate positions on the right side of your fabric. The distance between the two lines should be equal to the width of the lace you will be inserting. Cut away the fabric between these two lines and overlock or zigzag the two raw edges.

Working on the right side, and starting at a seam or outside edge, pin the lace into position so that 5 mm (¼ in) of the lace overlaps the finished edge of the project. Straight stitch into position along each overlocked or zigzagged edge, tucking the lace under at the end so that its raw edge is hidden (*see* Joining Ribbon and Lace, this page).

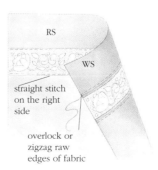

RS

WS

straight stitch
on the right
side

overlock or
zigzag raw
edges of fabric

FIGURE 5

MAKING PIPING

Piping, which creates an elegant finish, is usually inserted between the main section of an item and the frill, or stitched around the edges of an item. Buy your piping ready-made, or make your own in the fabric of your choice, as described below (*see* Figure 6).

You will need preshrunk piping cord and a length of fabric cut on the bias. Add 2.5 cm (1 in) to the diameter of the cord, and cut the strip of fabric to this width. With the wrong sides together, fold the strip of fabric around the cord so that the raw edges meet. Using the zipper or piping foot of your sewing machine, stitch the fabric closed to form a tube, as close as possible to the cord, so that the cord becomes enclosed in the tube. Trim the seam allowances to about 1 cm (⅜ in).

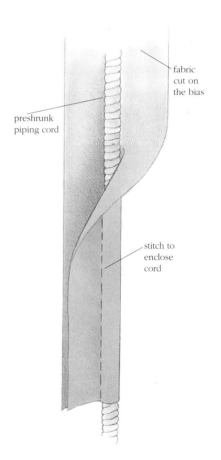

fabric
cut on
the bias

preshrunk
piping cord

stitch to
enclose
cord

FIGURE 6

CHAPTER ONE

SMALL PROJECTS

*C*ontained in this section is an interesting selection of small projects that will make a very effective addition to any room in the house, and a lovely gift for a special friend. Including a cover for a wastepaper bin, a lingerie bag, a mirror surround, a lampshade and a round tablecloth – to name a few – these projects are relatively straightforward and will provide an excellent introduction to making soft furnishings with calico. Many are small enough to be made out of offcuts left over from other projects.

WASTEPAPER
BIN COVER

*Nothing looks worse than a metal
wastepaper bin that has become
rusty, with peeling or faded paint!
Revamp your wastepaper bin (or buy
and decorate an inexpensive wicker
basket) by covering it with this
easy-to-make removable cover. To
protect the basket, line it with a
plastic bag – tucking the top of the
bag under the lip of the cover.*

REQUIREMENTS

a small metal or plastic wastepaper bin
or wicker wastepaper basket
calico (amount will depend on size of bin
or basket; *see* Steps 1 and 4 below)
matching cotton thread
14 mm-wide (½ in-wide) satin ribbon
2.5 cm-wide (1 in-wide) edging lace
about 50 cm x 2.5 cm-wide (20 in x
1 in-wide) satin ribbon, for the bow
eight-cord elastic

1. To determine how much fabric
you will need to cover the bin or
basket you have chosen, measure
its circumference at the widest
point and add 2 cm (¾ in) for seam
allowances. Measure the height
of the bin and add 10 cm (4 in) to
this measurement to allow for
casings. Cut a rectangle of fabric
using these measurements.

2. Fold the rectangle in half,
with right sides together, so that
its short sides meet. Join the long
sides of the new rectangle using
your overlocker or the straight
stitch of your sewing machine,
neatening the raw edges with
a zigzag stitch. Press the seam
open or to one side. You should
now have a tube, with the right
side of the fabric on the inside.

3. Turn 1 cm (⅜ in) and then a
further 1 cm (⅜ in) along one short
side of the tube to the wrong side
to form a casing about 1 cm
(⅜ in) wide. Press the casing into
position, then pin and stitch,

leaving an opening of about
2 cm (¾ in) before the side seam,
through which to thread the
elastic. Repeat this procedure
along the bottom edge. The tube
should now have a casing at
each end (*see* Figure 1).

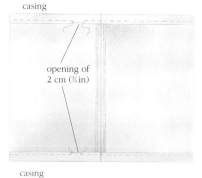

FIGURE 1

4. To make the frill, cut a strip of
calico 8 cm (3¼ in) in width and
double the circumference of the
bin at its widest point, in length.
If necessary, join strips of calico
using French seams (*see* Making
a French Seam, page 8) to obtain
the required length. Overlock or
zigzag one long side of the frill to
neaten. Gather the other long side
of the frill (*see* Gathering a Frill,
page 8) to fit the circumference
of the tube.

5. Turn the tube right side out and
draw a soft pencil line all the way
round, 8 cm (3¼ in) from the top
(refer to Figure 2 for the final
positioning of the frill). Then turn
the cover inside out again.

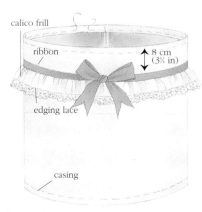

FIGURE 2

6. Starting at the side seam and
working on the inside (right side)
of the tube, place the gathered
edge of the frill right side up in
position along the pencil line, so
that your final stitching line will
coincide with the pencil line.
Carefully pin the frill into position
and stitch down, leaving about
2.5 cm (1 in) loose at each end.
Join the two loose ends of the frill
using a French seam (*see* Making
a French Seam, page 8) and
complete stitching.

7. Neaten the work and remove
any bulkiness by trimming away
the excess fabric above the stitch
line, leaving only about 5 mm
(¼ in) intact. Starting at the side
seam, pin the 14 mm-wide (½ in-
wide) satin ribbon neatly over the
raw edge of the frill, leaving an
extra 2 cm (¾ in) loose at one end.
Stitch the ribbon in position using
a row of straight stitches close to
each edge of the ribbon. Make a
neat join, folding the longer end
over and stitching it down securely
over the other end (*see* Joining
Ribbon and Lace, page 9). Do
not position this join on top of
other joins or seams, as it may
become rather bulky.

8. Turn the cover right side out
and stitch the edging lace along
the overlocked or zigzagged edge
of the frill, joining the ends of
the lace neatly and securely (*see*
Joining Ribbon and Lace, page 9).

9. Make a bow using the 2.5 cm-
wide (1 in-wide) satin ribbon and
sew it into position on the ribbon
on the side opposite the seam.

10. Thread the elastic through the
top and bottom casings (leaving
a fair amount of slack) and knot
loosely. Pull the cover over the
wastepaper bin or basket, then
tighten and knot the elastic so
that the cover fits snugly. Do not
tighten the top elastic too much, or
you will not be able to remove the

MAKING A FABRIC BOW

REQUIREMENTS

75 cm x 10 cm (29½ in x 4 in) calico
(or fabric in the colour or pattern of your choice)
matching cotton thread

1. With right sides of the fabric together, bring the short sides of the strip together, halving its length. Shape the ends diagonally, using the photographs on this page as a guide to determine your cutting angle.

2. Keeping the strip folded, mark off two points on the fold, 2.5 cm (1 in) from each raw edge. Starting at each of these points in turn, cut along the long sides of the strip towards the shaped ends, gradually widening to retain a width of 10 cm (4 in).

3. Unfold, overlock or zigzag raw edges, and make a narrow hem. Press.

TYING THE BOW

As this technique usually takes a little practice to perfect, it is a good idea to use a strip of scrap fabric to begin with. Once you have mastered twisting and tying the bow, use the hemmed strip of fabric.

4. Pick up the strip as shown at the top of the next column, roughly determining where the centre of the bow will be positioned once it has been tied. The shaping will assist you, but also take into account that the two ends of the bow should be more or less the same length to create a balanced look. Fold the fabric to form one half of the bow as shown, using your left hand to hold the fabric together at this central

point. The section of fabric which falls to the right now faces the wrong side. Take this in your right hand.

5. Twist your left wrist as shown below, so that the folded section of the bow (which was at the top) now points to the right, and its end points to the left. Bring the fabric in your right hand up and over the front of your left thumb, extending it over the top of your left hand as shown.

6. Holding the centre of the bow together between the thumb and forefinger of your left hand, lift the other fingers as shown below. Fold the fabric in your right hand down between the forefinger and middle finger of your left hand.

7. Twist your left wrist so that the palm faces you. The fabric falling to the right will have its wrong side facing you. Use your right hand to twist the strip to the right as shown at the top of the next column, so that the right side of the fabric faces you.

8. Now bring this strip towards you under your forefinger, folding it and threading the folded edge through the gap made by your left thumb. Gradually remove your thumb from the gap as you thread the fabric through.

9. Pull the folded section of fabric through the gap as far as necessary to balance the opposite half of the bow.

10. Work the fabric until you are happy with the shape of the bow. One end of the bow will be facing the wrong side. Simply twist it behind the central part of the bow so that its right side also faces the front.

11. Attach the bow in the required position, using small, neat stitches.

A simple wicker wastepaper basket has been given a pretty calico cover.

LINGERIE BAG

This is a wonderfully romantic and decorative accessory – something simple that always makes a perfect gift. It has many uses in the bedroom and the bathroom. Friends tell me that they use their bags for storing things like stockings, sleepwear, delicate silk undies, feminine unmentionables and even hair curlers!

REQUIREMENTS

2 pieces of calico, each measuring 65 cm x
35 cm (25½ in x 13¾ in)
65 cm x 35 cm (25½ in x 13¾ in)
compressed wadding
70 cm x 6 cm-wide (¾ yd x 2¼ in-wide)
edging lace
matching cotton thread
1 press stud or a short piece of Velcro
50 cm x 2.5 cm-wide (20 in x 1 in-wide)
satin ribbon, for the bow

1. Place one piece of calico on top of the other, with right sides together. Fold the fabric in half, halving its width (*see* Figure 1a), so that you have four layers of fabric. Now fold up the bottom third of the fabric as shown in Figure 1b. This will determine the depth of the bag.

cover to wash it. Cut off any excess elastic and arrange the gathers of the cover evenly all the way round.

VARIATIONS
❧ To make a very feminine cover, stitch a double row of lace or satin ribbon to the frill.

❧ Make a double frill by gathering wide lace and calico together. The lace should be about 2 cm (¾ in) narrower than the calico. Stitch

8 mm-wide (¼ in-wide) satin ribbon and edging lace to the edge of the bottom (calico) frill.

❧ Instead of satin ribbon and lace, use bias binding in the colour of your choice to finish the edges of the frill neatly.

❧ Instead of using a ribbon bow, make a pretty fabric bow (*see* Making a Fabric Bow, page 13) and sew it into position on the side opposite the seam.

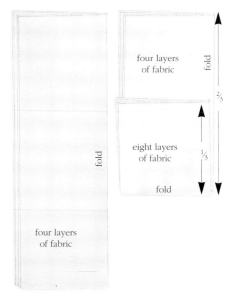

FIGURE 1A   FIGURE 1B

2. Keeping the fabric folded, shape the flap of the bag as shown in Figure 2. Use a dinner plate or a similar round object to obtain an even, semicircular shape. Draw an arc using a soft pencil and cut along the line through all four layers. Unfold the fabric.

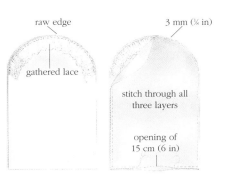

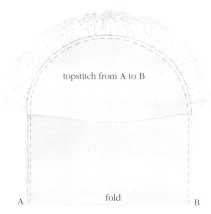

FIGURE 3   FIGURE 4

FIGURE 5

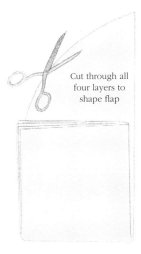

Cut through all four layers to shape flap

FIGURE 2

3. Keeping right sides together, place the two pieces of shaped calico on top of wadding. Cut wadding to same shape as calico.

4. Place one piece of calico on top of the wadding, right side up. With right sides together, and, if your lace has a raw edge, raw edges aligned, pin and stitch the gathered lace (*see* Gathering a Frill, page 8) to the curve (*see* Figure 3).

5. With right sides together, place the second piece of calico on top of the calico with the lace attached to it, keeping the lace folded towards the centre. Starting a short distance from the centre of the short, straight side, stitch through all three layers using a straight stitch. Work all the way round the edge, 3 mm (⅛ in) from the edge (*see* Figure 4), leaving an opening of about 15 cm (6 in) as indicated.

6. Turn the bag right side out, and press. Stitch the opening closed or sew it up by hand using small, neat slip stitches.

7. Fold the fabric to form the bag, bringing the short, straight side up to the start of the shaped flap. Pin the folded fabric into position and topstitch along the sides of the bag to close, about 3 mm (⅛ in) from the working edge, from A to B (*see* Figure 5).

8. Determine the correct position for the press stud or Velcro and sew into place. Use the 2.5 cm-wide (1 in-wide) satin ribbon to make a bow and sew it to the outside of the flap to cover any stitches that may be visible.

A Lingerie Bag containing a Potpourri Sachet (page 16) makes a lovely gift.

MAKING A POTPOURRI SACHET

Make a simple sachet filled with aromatic potpourri to put in your lingerie bag.

REQUIREMENTS

20 cm x 10 cm-wide (8 in x 4 in-wide) edging lace
matching cotton thread
20 cm x 2.5 cm-wide (8 in x 1 in-wide) satin ribbon

1. Fold the lace in half, with right sides together. Ensuring that the most decorative edge of the lace will form the top of the sachet, stitch up the bottom (from A to B) and the side (from B to C) using your overlocker or sewing machine (*see* Figure 1).

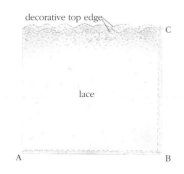

FIGURE 1

2. Turn the sachet right side out, fill about two-thirds full with potpourri and tie the ribbon securely around the top, making a decorative bow.

MIRROR SURROUND

Jazz up an ordinary mirror with this very effective, yet simple, slip-on surround that can be removed and washed, or choose a variation that suits your personal taste and the colour scheme of the room.

REQUIREMENTS

an oval mirror (*see* Note, below)
calico (amount will depend on size of mirror; *see* Steps 1 and 4, below)
matching cotton thread
14 mm-wide (½ in-wide) satin ribbon
2.5 cm-wide (1-in wide) edging lace
about 50 cm x 2.5 cm-wide (20 in x 1 in-wide) satin ribbon, for the bow
eight-cord elastic

NOTE   I used a mirror measuring 44 cm x 33 cm (17¼ in x 13 in) at its widest points – a size that is readily available from leading supermarkets and hardware stores – but almost any mirror will do.

1. Measure the circumference of the mirror and add 2 cm (¾ in) to this measurement for seam allowances. This will give you the length of fabric you need for the mirror surround. I usually find 12 cm (4¾ in) to be a good width. Cut out a strip of calico of the desired width and length.

2. With right sides together, fold the strip of calico in half so that its short sides meet. Stitch the short sides together to form a side

seam. Finish the raw edges of the seam off neatly by overlocking or zigzagging and then pressing.

3. Turn back 1 cm (⅜ in), and then a further 1 cm (⅜ in), to form a casing along one long side of the surround. Finger press or press, then pin and stitch using a straight stitch, leaving a gap of about 1.5 cm (⅝ in) just before the join to allow you to thread the elastic through. Repeat this procedure to make a casing along the other side (*see* Figure 1).

4. To make the frill, use a strip of calico double the circumference of the mirror in length and 6 cm (2¼ in) in width. If necessary, join several strips of calico using French seams (*see* Making a French Seam, page 8) to obtain the required length. Overlock or zigzag one long side of the frill and gather the other long side (*see* Gathering a Frill, page 8) to fit the mirror surround.

5. Position the fabric for the mirror surround right side up. Pin the frill (right side up) into position about 1 cm (⅜ in) away from the inside stitching line, starting at the join of the surround (*see* Figure 2 on the next page). Leaving about 2.5 cm (1 in) of the frill loose at each end, stitch the frill into position. Join the two loose ends of the frill using a French seam (*see* Making a French Seam, page 8) and complete stitching.

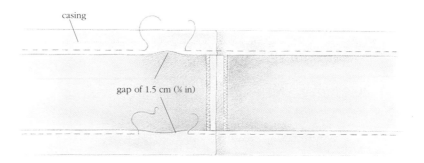

casing

gap of 1.5 cm (⅝ in)

FIGURE 1

16

Satin ribbon and a double lace frill decorate this Mirror Surround (page 16).

6. Neaten the work and trim away the excess fabric above the stitching line, leaving only about 5 mm (¼ in) intact. Starting at the join, stitch 14 mm-wide (½ in-wide) ribbon neatly over the raw edge of the frill using a row of straight stitches close to each edge of the ribbon. Allow one end of the ribbon to overlap the other by about 2 cm (¾ in); fold under and secure with a row of neat stitches (*see* Joining Ribbon and Lace, page 9). Position this join about 2 cm (¾ in) away from the join on the fabric surround.

7. Stitch the edging lace to the overlocked or zigzagged edge of the frill, joining the ends (*see* Joining Ribbon and Lace, page 9).

8. Make a bow using the 2.5 cm-wide (1 in-wide) ribbon and sew the bow to the ribbon on the side opposite the joins.

9. Thread the elastic through the top and bottom casings (leaving a fair amount of slack), and knot loosely. Pull the surround over the mirror and rotate it so that the ribbon bow is positioned centrally at the bottom of the mirror. Tighten the elastic so that the surround fits the mirror snugly, and knot securely. Cut off any excess elastic and arrange the gathers evenly all the way round.

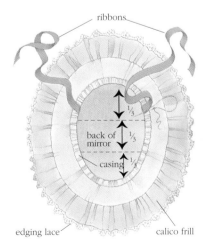

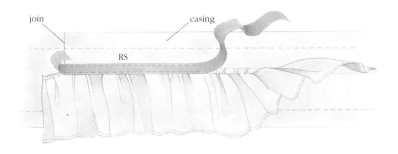

FIGURE 2

FIGURE 3

10. Cut two pieces of 14 mm-wide (½ in-wide) ribbon, each about 30 cm (12 in) in length. Turn the mirror over and neatly sew a piece of ribbon into position on the back of the surround, about one third of the way down from the top of the mirror on each side (*see* Figure 3, page 17). Note that these ribbons need to be attached very securely, as they will be tied together to form a bow that will be used to suspend the mirror.

VARIATIONS

❧ To make a very feminine mirror surround, stitch a double row of lace or ribbon to the frill.

❧ Make an attractive double frill for the mirror surround by gathering 6 cm-wide (2¼ in-wide) edging lace with your 6 cm-wide (2¼ in-wide) calico frill. Position the lace frill on top of the calico frill, and stitch narrow edging lace along the edge of the calico frill so that it protrudes beyond the edge of the lace frill above it. This creates a lovely, full effect.

❧ Stitch bias binding in the colour of your choice to the mirror surround instead of ribbon; attach bias binding in a contrasting colour to the edge of the frill instead of lace; and make a fabric bow in the colour of your choice instead of a ribbon bow (*see* Making a Fabric Bow, page 13).

A pretty, covered basket is not only decorative, but can also be useful for storing odds and ends.

BASKET COVER

An old, neglected basket can easily be made to look like new with a pretty calico cover and lid. Use a large, sturdy basket to hold magazines that lie around the house, or to store family board games or Mother's knitting. Smaller 'keep-it-tidy' baskets are useful for storing hair accessories on a dressing table, extra toilet rolls in the bathroom, or cotton wool, baby powder and lotions in the nursery.

REQUIREMENTS

a basket with a handle and a solid, flat base made of hardboard
calico (amount will depend on the size and the shape of the basket; *see* Steps 1, 8, 14 and 16, below)
matching cotton thread
scrap paper for template
2.5 cm-wide (1 in-wide) edging lace
eight-cord elastic
14 mm-wide (½ in-wide) satin ribbon
compressed wadding (amount will depend on the size and shape of the basket)
2.5 cm-wide (1 in-wide) satin ribbon

NOTE The basket cover consists of two parts. The first part lines the inside of the basket, folds over the lip and ends in a frill on the outside. The second part is a decorative lid. The same rules apply for measuring and cutting, whether you're covering a round, square or rectangular basket.

FRILLED LINING

1. To determine the length of the fabric you need, measure the circumference of the basket at its widest point and multiply this measurement by 1.5. To determine the width of the fabric, place the beginning of the tape measure on the inside of the basket touching the base, run it up over the lip and down the outside, until you reach the desired length of the frill (*see* Figure 1, measuring from A to B). Decide at this point whether you

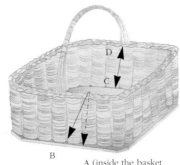

FIGURE 1

A (inside the basket on the base)

want the frill to cover the entire basket, or whether you want the wicker at the base to be visible.

2. Cut the fabric to the required measurements and fold in half, halving the length measurement. Cut the fabric along the fold line, so that you have two pieces of fabric of the same size.

3. Overlock or zigzag one long side and both short sides of each of the two pieces of fabric.

4. Return to the basket and measure the inside height, from the base to just below the lip (*see* Figure 1, measuring from C to D).

5. Place the two pieces of fabric together, right sides together, with the long overlocked or zigzagged sides at the top. Using the inside height measurement from Step 4, mark this position along each short side of the fabric using pins (*see* Figure 2).

6. Make two side seams, stitching up to the level of the pins on each side. Press the seams open, neatening and securing them all the way along with an additional

two pieces of fabric for frilled lining RS together

inside height of basket

FIGURE 2

row of stitching, as shown in Figure 3. You should now have a wide tube of fabric.

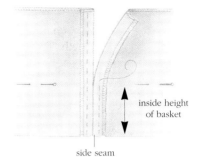

FIGURE 3

inside height of basket

side seam

7. Gather the raw edge of the tube all the way round (*see* Gathering a Frill, page 8).

8. Place the basket on a piece of paper and draw a pencil line on the paper, all the way round the base, staying close to the edge of the basket. Cut out two identical pieces of calico for the base of the cover using this template. Use pins to mark the position of the handles on one piece of calico.

9. With right sides together, pin the gathered edge of the tube, along its circumference, to one of the fabric bases (with the handle positions marked). Line up each seam in the tube with a handle position (*see* Figure 4). Stitch down neatly all round.

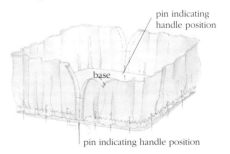

pin indicating handle position

base

pin indicating handle position

FIGURE 4

10. Keeping the tube folded towards the centre, place the other base piece, right side down, on top of the tube. Pin and stitch into position, leaving an opening of 10–15 cm (4–6 in). Turn the

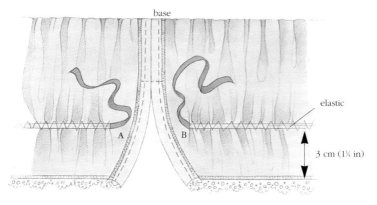

FIGURE 5

work to the right side through the opening. On the base, close the opening by tucking in the edges and stitching together neatly and securely by hand.

11. Working on the right side of the fabric, stitch 2.5 cm-wide (1 in-wide) edging lace to the two overlocked or zigzagged bottom edges of the frill, finishing off and securing the ends neatly.

12. Working along a line about 3 cm (1¼ in) from the lace, and starting 1 cm (⅜ in) from each seam edge, zigzag or straight stitch 8-cord elastic to the wrong side of each side of the frill, stretching it slightly as you sew (*see* Figure 5 at the top of the page).

13. Finally, firmly stitch about 15 cm (6 in) of 14 mm-wide (½ in-wide) ribbon to each side of the frill, at the start and finish of the elastic on each side of the frill (*see* points A and B on Figure 5). These two pairs of ribbons will ultimately form the ties that will hold the frill in place around the basket.

LID

14. To calculate how much fabric you need to make the main part of the lid, measure the width and length of the top of the basket at its widest points. Using these measurements, cut out two squares or rectangles of calico and one of wadding, adding a 1 cm (⅜ in) seam allowance all round to the calico.

15. Quilt one layer of calico and wadding together lightly. The function of the quilting is simply to hold the wadding and the calico together, so in fact very little quilting is necessary (*see* Figure 6). (I also find that heavy quilting tends to distort the shape.) Decorate the quilted layer with 2.5 cm-wide (1 in-wide) ribbon and lace in any way you like. Place this decorated layer in position on the basket, use pins to mark the position of the handles and trim the lid carefully to fit the shape of the top of the basket, still allowing 1 cm (⅜ in) all round on the calico for seams.

FIGURE 6

16. The frill for the lid is made in two pieces so as to accommodate the handles. To calculate the length of each piece, measure the circumference of the basket at its widest point (this is to allow for gathering). If necessary, join strips of calico using French seams (*see* Making a French Seam, page 8)

to obtain the required length. The width of the frill will depend on personal preference and the size of the basket. I usually recommend a frill width of about 4 cm (1½ in). Cut out the pieces.

17. Overlock or zigzag one long side of each of the two frill pieces. Gather the other long side of each piece to fit about half the circumference of the lid (*see* Gathering a Frill, page 8).

18. Pin each of the two gathered frill pieces into position on the lid (right sides together), starting next to the marked position of the handles (*see* Figure 7). Stitch down, allowing space for the handles and making sure that you turn over a small hem (to the wrong side) at the beginning and end of each piece. Stitch a 15 cm (6 in) length of 14-mm wide (½ in-wide) ribbon securely at the four points to form ties (*see* Figure 7, points A, B, C and D).

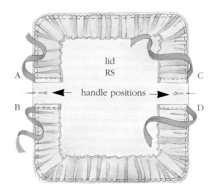

FIGURE 7

19. Place the remaining piece of fabric for the lid on top of the other piece (right sides together), keeping the gathered frill folded towards the centre. Pin the loose piece into position and stitch down all round, leaving an opening of 10 cm (4 in). Turn the work right side out and sew the opening closed.

20. Stitch 2.5 cm-wide (1 in-wide) edging lace to the right side of the overlocked or zigzagged edge

of the frill, joining the ends (*see* Joining Ribbon and Lace, page 9).

21. Pull the elasticated frill of the cover over the upper lip of the basket, smoothing the remaining part down to line the basket neatly. Tie the ribbon pairs on either side into bows to hold the frill in position. Place the lid in position and tie the ribbon pairs into bows around the handles.

TISSUE BOX COVER

For many people there is nothing worse than a bare, cardboard tissue box. A pretty cover on a tissue box in the guest room, for instance, adds a special finishing touch.

REQUIREMENTS

a tissue box with the opening at the front
calico (amount will depend on size of box;
see Steps 1 and 2, below)
wadding (amount will depend on size of box;
see Step 2, below)
matching cotton thread
2.5 cm-wide (1 in-wide) edging lace
20 cm x 8 mm-wide (8 in x ⅜ in-wide)
satin ribbon, for the bow

1. You will need to cut one large piece of fabric to cover three of the long sides of the box and two smaller pieces to cover the two small sides. Refer to Figure 1 and measure lines AB, CD, EF and GH of your tissue box. Write down these measurements, adding 2 cm (¾ in) to each measurement for seam allowances.

2. Using the measurement for AB as the width, and that for CD as the length, cut out one large piece of calico to cover the central part of the box (i.e. three of the long sides). Now cut out two smaller pieces, each with EF and GH as dimensions, for the sides. Cut out three pieces of wadding, slightly bigger than each calico piece.

A Tissue Box Cover can be as simple or as fancy as you like.

3. Quilt the relevant pieces of calico and wadding together lightly. The function of the quilting is simply to hold the wadding and the calico together, so in fact very little real quilting is necessary. Refer to Figure 2a on page 22 for guidance on quilting the central part of the cover, and to Figure 2b for the sides.

4. Decorate the central part of the cover using a strip of edging lace along each side of the box (*see* Figure 3, page 22), positioning it about 5 cm (2 in) from the outer edge. Add satin ribbon if you like.

5. With right sides together, join the central panel to one of the side

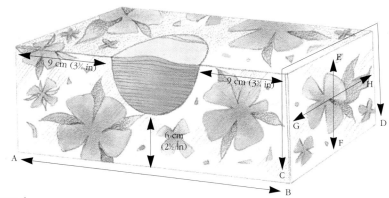

FIGURE 1

9 cm (3¾ in)
9 cm (3¾ in)
6 cm (2½ in)

21

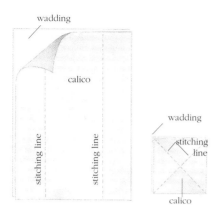

FIGURE 2A   FIGURE 2B

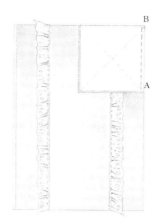

FIGURE 4A

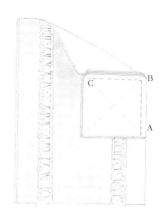

FIGURE 4B

panels, referring to Figures 4a–c. Start by stitching from A to B, then swing the work around, stitch from B to C, swing the work around again, and then stitch from C to D.

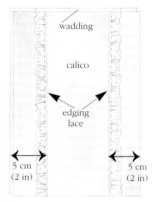

FIGURE 3

Repeat the procedure to join the second side panel (on the other side). Remove any bulkiness from the seams on the inside of the work by snipping away excess fabric and tidying the edges. Overlock or zigzag all around the bottom edge.

6. Place the cover over the box and use a soft pencil to mark the position of the hole on the right side of the fabric. The hole should be big enough to allow easy access to the tissues, but ensure that none of the cardboard box will be visible. Trace off Figure 5 and use it as a template; use Figure 1 as a guide to positioning it correctly.

Cut an oval hole in the fabric and carefully overlock or zigzag around the raw edge.

7. Gather the 2.5 cm-wide (1 in-wide) edging lace to fit the circumference of the hole using a strip that is double the circumference of the hole in length (*see* Gathering a Frill, page 8). Pin the lace into position, beginning at the centre of the lower edge of the hole. Neatly stitch the lace down all round the circle, leaving about 2 cm (¾ in) loose at the beginning and the end. Join the ends of the lace at the centre of the lower edge of the hole (*see* Joining Ribbon and Lace, page 9), pin and complete stitching.

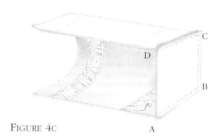

FIGURE 4C   A

8. Make a small, 8 mm-wide (⅜ in-wide) ribbon bow and sew it to the centre of the lower edge of the hole to decorate the cover and hide the join in the lace.

VARIATION
❧ Use bias binding in the colour of your choice instead of lace around the circle and around the bottom edge of the cover.

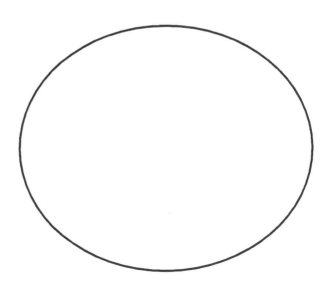

FIGURE 5

A Round Tablecloth with a Frill covers the bedside table, and is topped with a frilled Decorative Overlay (page 25).

ROUND TABLECLOTH WITH A FRILL

Small, round tables are a good choice for filling empty corners in almost any room. They can be made to look very pretty, and offer useful surface space for displaying treasured objects like favourite family photographs. Use a small, round table in the living room, next to the bed, for the telephone or even in the bathroom. Draped with a lovely, floor-length tablecloth and a decorative overlay, it can add a special finishing touch.

REQUIREMENTS

calico (amount will depend on diameter and height of table; *see* Steps 1 and 5, below)
matching cotton thread

1. You'll need to begin with a large square of fabric. To calculate its measurements (*see* Figure 1), first measure the diameter of the table (measurement X). Now measure the drop from the edge of the table to the floor or to the lowest point you would like the cloth to reach (measurement Y). Multiply measurement Y by 2 and add this to measurement X, i.e.

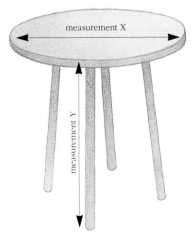

FIGURE 1

(Y x 2) + X. The total will give you the measurement for each side of the square. If you want to make a tablecloth with a frill, decide on the depth of the frill and subtract this from the measurement for the main section of the tablecloth.

2. Cut a square of fabric to the required size and fold it in half, with right sides together, and in half again, so that you have a square consisting of four layers of fabric, that is now a quarter of the size of the original square that you cut out.

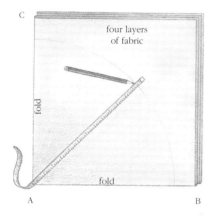

C

four layers
of fabric

fold

fold

A   B

FIGURE 2

3. Use a tape measure to mark out an arc on the top quarter of the fabric. To do this, hold the tape measure firmly in the inner corner of the folded fabric (*see* Figure 2, point A). Pull the tape measure taut and measure one side of the small square (from point A to point B). The distance from A to B should be the same as the distance from A to C – this is the radius of your circle. Keeping the tape measure firmly in place at point A, and keeping it taut, slowly rotate it all the way across the square from point B to point C, marking off several points the same distance from point A as point B as you go. Remove the tape measure and use a soft pencil line to join the points that you have marked off between B and C to form an arc.

4. Keeping the fabric folded, cut along the arc you have drawn, through all four layers. This should give you a near perfect circle when you unfold the fabric.

5. To calculate the length of fabric needed for the frill, multiply the circumference of the circle by 2. Cut the required number of strips for the frill to total this length when joined, and to the width of your choice (*see* Step 1).

6. You will need to join strips of fabric to make the frill the required length (*see* Making a French Seam, page 8) and you will need to work with great care when gathering and attaching it to the main part of the cloth. I usually recommend marking off four points with equal distances between them on both the frill and the outer edge of the tablecloth. Then zigzag or overlock one long side of the frill. Gather the other side of the frill (*see* Gathering a Frill, page 8), working separately with each of the four parts you have measured off. Now line up the four points on the gathered frill with the four points marked off on the main part of the tablecloth. Working this way will ensure that the gathers are evenly spaced around the circumference, not bunched in any one section.

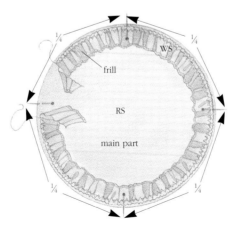

¼   ¼

WS

frill

RS

main part

¼   ¼

FIGURE 3

7. With the right sides of the main part of the tablecloth and the frill together, pin the gathered edge of the frill into position all along the edge of the circle (*see* Figure 3). Leaving about 2.5 cm (1 in) of the frill loose at the beginning and the end, stitch it down all round. Join the ends of the frill neatly using a French seam (*see* Making a French Seam, page 8) and complete stitching.Overlock or zigzag raw edges to neaten.

8. Working on the right side of the central piece of the tablecloth, not the frill, topstitch neatly 5 mm (¼ in) from the seam line, so that the seam lies flat (*see* Figure 4). Hem the bottom edge of the frill.

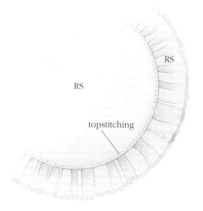

RS

RS

topstitching

FIGURE 4

VARIATIONS
❦ When making a frilled tablecloth, gather 8 cm-wide (3¼ in-wide) lace with the fabric frill to form a double frill, with the lace lying on top of the fabric frill.

❦ For a simple, elegant finish, use bias binding in a contrasting colour along the bottom edge of the tablecloth instead of the frill.

❦ You may wish to add some pretty ribbon bows to your tablecloth. I sometimes use four 2.5 cm-wide (1 in-wide) ribbon bows and space them evenly around the circumference of the cloth, positioning them just above the seam line of the frill.

DECORATIVE OVERLAY

Small, round bedside tables are becoming increasingly popular. Give yours a smart, finished look using a decorative calico overlay over a plain, floor-length tablecloth.

REQUIREMENTS

NOTE   The measurements and list of requirements given here are appropriate for a table with a diameter of 50 cm (20 in), but can be adapted for smaller or larger tables. As the length of the overhang is variable, experiment with different sizes and determine a suitable size by trial and error.

82 cm x 150 cm-wide (32¼ in x 59 in-wide) calico

matching cotton thread

2 m x 14 mm-wide (2⅛ yd x ½ in-wide) satin ribbon

4 m x 2.5 cm-wide (4⅜ yd x 1 in-wide) edging lace

2 m x 2.5 cm-wide (2⅛ yd x 1 in-wide) satin ribbon, for the bows

This simple Decorative Overlay uses contrast piping and Fabric Bows (page 13).

1. For the main part of the overlay you will need a square of fabric measuring 82 cm x 82 cm (32¼ in x 32¼ in). For the frill you will need a strip of fabric 8 cm (3¼ in) wide and about 4 m (4⅜ yd) in length. If necessary, join strips of calico, using French seams (*see* Making a French Seam, page 8), to obtain the required length.

2. Overlock or zigzag the edges of the square; turn 1 cm (⅜ in) to the wrong side all round and stitch to hem. Overlock or zigzag one long side of the frill and gather the other (*see* Gathering a Frill, page 8).

3. Fold the square in half, with right sides together, and in half again, so that it is a quarter of its original size.

4. Use a tape measure to help you draw an arc with a radius of 30 cm (12 in) on the top quarter of the

fabric. To do this, refer to the technique described in Step 3 on page 24. Hold the tape measure in position firmly on the inner corner of the folded fabric. Pull the tape measure taut and rotate it to mark off two points 30 cm (12 in) from the centre point, along each of the relevant sides of the square. Holding the tape measure firmly in place in the corner, and keeping it

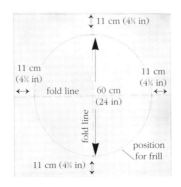

FIGURE 1

taut, slowly rotate it all the way across the square once more, marking off several points at the 30 cm-mark (12 in-mark) as you go. Remove the tape measure and use a soft pencil line to join the points to form an arc.

5. Keeping the fabric folded, simply turn it over so that the quarter that was at the bottom is now on top. Repeat Step 4 to draw an arc on this quarter. If you open up the fabric, you should see the semicircle that you have drawn.

6. Fold the fabric again, exposing the quarters on which you have not yet drawn. Now draw an arc on each of them in the same way as before. You should now have drawn a complete circle. THIS IS NOT A CUTTING LINE – it shows the position of the frill (*see* Figure 1).

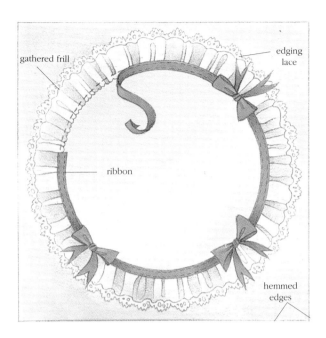

gathered frill

edging lace

ribbon

hemmed edges

FIGURE 2

7. Open the square to its full size, right side up. Take the gathered frill, right side up, and pin into position all along the circle you have drawn. Leaving about 2.5 cm (1 in) of the frill loose at the beginning and the end, stitch it down all round. Join the ends of the frill neatly using a French seam (*see* Making a French Seam, page 8) and complete stitching.

8. Remove bulkiness by trimming away any excess fabric above the stitching line, leaving only about 5 mm (¼ in) intact. Cover the raw edge of the frill with 14 mm-wide (½ in-wide) satin ribbon. Pin the ribbon into position, allowing one end to overlap the other slightly. Fold the overlap over and make a neat join (*see* Joining Ribbon and Lace, page 9). Stitch the ribbon down all round, using a row of straight stitches close to each edge of the ribbon (*see* Figure 2).

9. Stitch 2.5 cm-wide (1 in-wide) edging lace all along the bottom edge of the frill. Make four ribbon

bows from 2.5 cm-wide (1 in-wide) ribbon and sew them to the ribbon surround in the positions indicated in Figure 2.

VARIATIONS

❧ Use bias binding instead of ribbon to finish the raw edge of the frill, and fabric bows (*see* Making a Fabric Bow, page 13) instead of ribbon bows.

❧ Make a beautifully feminine double frill by gathering a long strip of wide lace with the calico frill, so that the lace frill lies on top of the calico frill.

❧ To create a very feminine appeal, use a double row of lace or ribbon in place of a single row.

❧ Sew bows to the four corners of the overlay below the frill, instead of on the ribbon surround. Choose 2.5 cm-wide (1 in-wide) ribbon bows or make larger bows from calico or fabric in the colour of your choice (*see* Making a Fabric Bow, page 13).

beginning with Step 2 on page 24.

HOW TO MAKE A ROUND TABLECLOTH WITHOUT A FRILL

People often ask me where to position the join when they are making a large, round tablecloth without a frill, using fabric that is narrower than the required diameter. The instructions below are a guide to making a tablecloth with a diameter of 180 cm (71 in), using calico that is 150 cm (59 in) wide, but can be adapted for making tablecloths of any size using fabric of any width.

REQUIREMENTS

1.8 m x 150 cm-wide (2 yd x 59 in-wide) calico
1.8 m x 32 cm (71 in x 12½ in) calico
matching cotton thread

Leaving a seam allowance of 1 cm (⅜ in), join the longest sides of the two pieces of calico (*see* Figure 1) to form a square measuring 180 cm x 180 cm (71 in x 71 in). Continue from here as for the Round Tablecloth with a Frill, beginning with Step 2 on page 24. Omit the frill, overlocking and hemming the edge of the cloth, or attaching bias binding in the colour of your choice to the neatened edge. Position the cloth over the table with the join facing the wall or where it will be least obvious. You'll be amazed at how little of the join is visible.

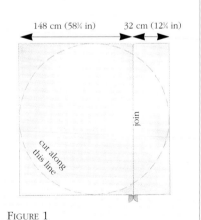

148 cm (58¼ in)   32 cm (12¼ in)

cut along this line

join

FIGURE 1

LAMPSHADE

Creative lighting can transform an otherwise dull room into an interesting one with atmosphere. It amazes me that people often ignore this very important fact when decorating their homes. I love frilly lampshades – they are pretty, functional and practical in the sense that they can be washed with ease. The frames I use are commonly known as Tiffany frames and can be purchased from most craft and decorating shops. As Tiffany frames come in different sizes depending on the manufacturer, your requirements may differ from mine. The following guidelines will help you determine your exact requirements, whatever the size of the frame you are using.

REQUIREMENTS

epoxy-coated Tiffany lampshade frame
calico (amount will depend on the size of the
lampshade frame; *see* Steps 1 and 4, below)
matching cotton thread
14 mm-wide (½ in-wide) satin ribbon
2.5 cm-wide (1 in-wide) edging lace
2.5 cm-wide (1 in-wide) satin ribbon for bows
eight-cord elastic

1. To determine the length of the fabric you need, measure the circumference of the frame at its widest point (not at the bottom) and add 2 cm (¾ in) to this measurement for seam allowances.

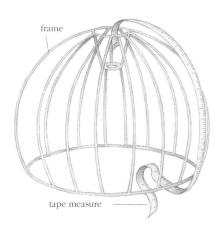

frame

tape measure

FIGURE 1

A wide lace frill and a lace insert in a Lampshade create a lovely effect.

To determine the width, fold your tape measure over the upper ring of the frame by about 2 cm (¾ in), bring it all the way down the side, fold it under the bottom ring of the frame by about 3 cm (1¼ in) (*see* Figure 1) and add 2 cm (¾ in) to this measurement for each casing. Cut out a rectangle of the required size.

2. Fold the rectangle of calico in half, right sides together, so that its short sides meet, and use your overlocker or a straight stitch on your sewing machine to stitch a side seam, forming the rectangle into a tube. Neaten the raw edges of the seam by overlocking or zigzagging, and press.

3. Keeping the right side of the fabric on the inside, turn the top edge of the tube outwards, folding it over by 1 cm (⅜ in), and then by a further 1 cm (⅜ in), to form a casing. Finger press or press the casing, then pin and stitch, ensuring that you accommodate the width of the elastic. Leave an opening of about 2 cm (¾ in) before the side seam to allow you to thread the elastic through. Repeat with the bottom edge of the tube.

4. To make the frill, cut a strip of calico 8 cm (3¼ in) in width and double the circumference of the frame at its widest point, in length. If necessary, join strips of calico to obtain the required length using French seams (*see* Making a French Seam, page 8). Overlock or zigzag one long side of the frill and gather the other side to fit the circumference of the lampshade (*see* Gathering a Frill, page 8).

5. Turn the calico tube right side out. Bearing in mind that you have made allowance for the lampshade cover to tuck under by 3 cm (1¼ in) and you would like the frill to hang just on the bottom edge of the frame, draw a soft pencil line 10 cm (4 in) from the bottom of the cover all the way round.

6. Turn the cover inside out and work along the pencil line, which is now on the inside. Starting at the side seam, place the raw edge of the frill right side up along the pencil line and pin into position. Your final stitching line should coincide with the pencil line. Leave about 2.5 cm (1 in) of the frill loose at each end and stitch down the frill. Join the loose ends of the frill using a French seam (*see* Making a French Seam, page 8) and complete stitching.

7. Neaten the work and remove any bulkiness by trimming away the excess fabric above the stitch line, leaving about 5 mm (¼ in) intact. Starting at the side seam, stitch the 14 mm-wide (½ in-wide) ribbon neatly over the raw edge of the frill using a row of straight stitches close to each edge of the ribbon. Allow one end of the ribbon to overlap the other by about 2 cm (¾ in), fold under, and secure with a row of neat stitches (*see* Joining Ribbon and Lace, page 9). It is better not to position this join exactly over the other seams, as it may become rather bulky.

8. Turn the cover right side out and stitch 2.5 cm-wide (1 in-wide) edging lace along the overlocked or zigzagged edge of the frill, joining the ends of the lace securely (*see* Joining Ribbon and Lace, page 9).

9. Make a bow using the 2.5 cm-wide (1 in-wide) ribbon and sew the bow into position on the ribbon on the side opposite the seam. You can use several bows of the same size spread out evenly around the circumference of the lampshade if you like, depending on its size. On a small bedside shade I usually use only one small bow, but in the right setting large bows can also look very attractive.

10. Thread elastic through the top and bottom casings (leaving a fair amount of slack) and knot loosely. Pull the cover over the frame. Now pull the top elastic in quite tightly and then pull in the bottom elastic so that the cover fits the frame snugly. Knot the elastic firmly and cut off any excess.

WASHING THE LAMPSHADE

You do not need to remove the cover from the frame for washing. Place the lampshade in a bath of lukewarm water and wash down using a soapy sponge. Rinse

thoroughly and use string to suspend it from the washing line. On a sunny day with a slight breeze it will be dry in no time at all. If you have not used an epoxy-coated frame to begin with, and your frame begins to rust, touch up rust spots using clear varnish.

VARIATIONS

❧ Decorate the dome of the cover using several rows of pin tucks (*see* Making Pin Tucks, page 9), lace and ribbon (*see* Figure 2).

❧ Insert lace (*see* Inserting Lace, page 9) in the dome of the cover (*see* photograph, page 27) after stitching up the side seam to form a tube. Depending on the size of the frame you are covering, allow 3–6 cm (1¼–2¼ in) from the top of the frame and insert 8 cm-wide (3¼ in-wide) lace, cutting out enough calico to make a gap that will accommodate the lace. When the lamp is being used, the light shining through the lace forms patterned shadows on the ceiling.

❧ On larger frames a double frill looks good, but bear in mind that the space between the two frills should not be too wide. I generally suggest using two frills, each about 8 cm (3¼ in) in width, placed about 3 cm (1¼ in) apart (*see* Figure 2).

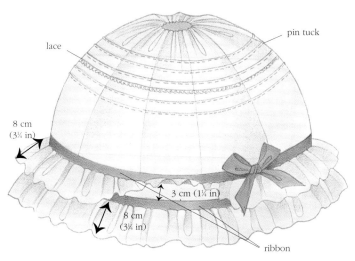

FIGURE 2

PADDED BOW

I stumbled upon the idea of making a padded bow when I was looking for a pretty, but simple and practical way of decorating the chairs in a restaurant. I had used shaped, boxed cushions held in place by thin ties. When I looked at the chairs, I decided they needed something decorative to hide the zip and the ties. I experimented with a variety of fabric bows, but they all seemed limp and uninspiring – not creating the effect I wanted to achieve. Then I thought of padding the bows and – after trying about 20 different variations – found the perfect answer. I now have the ideal decorative touch for dressing up bedposts, tied-back curtains, or the backs of chairs.

REQUIREMENTS

46 cm x 150 cm-wide (½ yd x 59 in-wide) calico
1.5 m x 90 cm-wide (1⅝ yd x 36 in-wide) compressed wadding (*see* Note, below)
matching cotton thread
20 cm (8 in) Velcro

Use a Padded Bow to decorate a simple chair for a festive occasion.

NOTE   You will use a strip of wadding that is only 18 cm (7 in) wide and 150 cm (59 in) in length, but you will need to buy 1.5 m (1⅝ yd) of wadding to avoid having a join. I do not recommend joining strips of wadding, as this can become quite bulky and unsightly if it is not done carefully. If, for some reason, you have to join strips of wadding, make sure that the join is placed at the centre of the bow when it is folded.

1. Cut a strip of calico measuring 36 cm x 150 cm (14 in x 59 in) and fold it in half, right sides together, so that you have a strip 18 cm (7 in) wide.

2. Cut one short side of the fabric diagonally, as shown in Figure 1. Pick up the side you have just cut and fold the fabric in half (*see* Figure 2) to guide shaping on the other side. Cut the other short side to match the first.

3. Keeping the fabric folded, shape the centre of the bow by cutting away the fabric from A to B as shown in Figure 2.

4. Unfold the fabric once only (so that its width is still halved) to open the strip out to its full length, and place it on the wadding. Cut the wadding to the same size and shape as the calico (i.e. a long strip no wider than 18 cm [7 in] and no longer than 150 cm [59 in]).

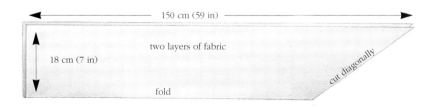

FIGURE 1

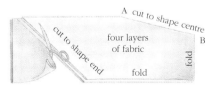

FIGURE 2

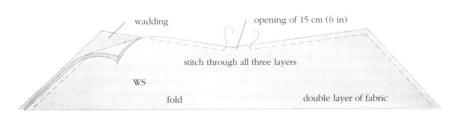

wadding

opening of 15 cm (6 in)

stitch through all three layers

WS

fold

double layer of fabric

FIGURE 3

5. Place the double layer of fabric, right sides together, on top of the wadding. Stitch through all three layers as shown in Figure 3, starting at the short sides and stitching upwards and then inwards towards the centre. Leave an opening of about 15 cm (6 in) in the centre as shown.

6. Turn the work right side out through the opening and press. Slipstitch the opening closed.

7. You now need two bands: a short, central band to hold the bow together, and a longer band which is used to attach the bow where you want it. The length of the longer band will depend on how and where you will be using your bow (i.e. to dress the back of a chair, or to decorate a tied-back curtain). To make the bands, cut two strips of calico, one measuring 16 cm x 10 cm (6¼ in x 4 in), and the other measuring 60 cm x 10 cm (24 in x 4 in).

8. Fold each strip in half, right sides together, and stitch up the long sides so that you have a tube. Turn right sides out, and press so that the join lies in the centre at the back of the strip (*see* Figure 4).

Fold the short sides in and slipstitch to close. Stitch a short strip of Velcro to each end of the longer band (*see* Figure 7).

9. To fold the main part of the bow, first mark the centre point of the shaped, padded strip using a pin. Place the strip on a flat surface in the position shown (*see* Figure 5a), with the longer of the long sides at the bottom. Bring the

pointed end on the right across to the left, and take the pointed end on the left across to the right (*see* Figure 5b). Wrap the band without the Velcro around the centre of the folded, padded strip to clinch it neatly (*see* Figure 6), and slipstitch to secure at the back.

10. Thread the band with the Velcro through the back of the centre band (*see* Figure 7) and secure the bow to the chair, bedpost or wherever you please.

VARIATIONS
❧ After completing Step 6, stitch narrow crochet lace around the edges of the bow.

❧ Use fabric in the colour of your choice to form the central band of a padded calico bow.

WS   join   RS

FIGURE 4

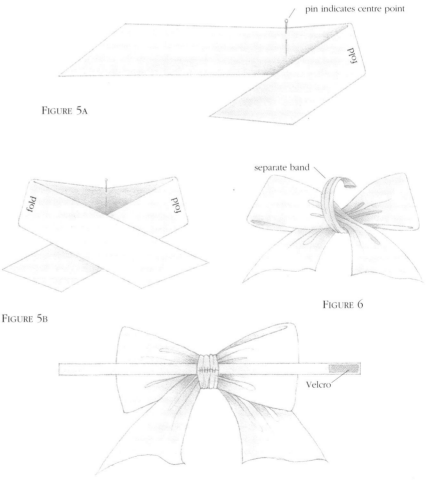

pin indicates centre point

fold

FIGURE 5A

fold   fold

FIGURE 5B

separate band

FIGURE 6

Velcro

FIGURE 7

SCATTER CUSHIONS

Piled on a couch or bed, or in deep armchairs, scatter cushions immediately create an atmosphere that is both inviting and informal. There are many variations of the basic scatter cushion; use your imagination, but always remember to keep to the decorative style of the rest of the room.

FRILLED SCATTER CUSHION COVER WITH PIN TUCKS, LACE AND RIBBON

This very basic square scatter cushion cover can be as simple or as complicated and decorative as you like. Follow my instructions or use your imagination and play around with the lace and satin ribbon.

REQUIREMENTS

70 cm x 150 cm-wide (¾ yd x 59 in-wide) calico

matching cotton thread

1.5 m x 14 mm-wide (1⅝ yd x ½ in-wide) satin ribbon

1.5 m x 2.5 cm-wide (1⅝ yd x 1 in-wide) edging lace

1. Cut out a square of calico measuring 42 cm x 42 cm (16½ in x 16½ in). Fold it in half, and in half again, so that you have four layers. Use an iron to press neatly, so that when you open the square, there is a cross shape in the centre.

2. Make the first pin tuck along one of the central lines (*see* Figure 1, line AD) of the cross (*see* Making Pin Tucks, page 9). I usually make each pin tuck about 3 mm (⅛ in) wide. Now measure about 3 cm (1 ¼ in) from the first pin tuck on either side and draw a

line parallel to the first pin tuck in these positions (*see* Figure 1). Make two further pin tucks, one along each of the pencil lines you have drawn (lines BE and CF).

3. Repeat this procedure, making another three pin tucks that cross those you have just made at a 90° angle (central line JG, then lines KH and LI). Ensure that the pin tucks all face the same direction where they cross (i.e. all lie to the right, for instance, as in Figure 1).

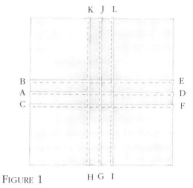

FIGURE 1

Three variations of the basic Frilled Scatter Cushion Cover, using pin tucks, lace and satin ribbon in different ways.

SCATTER CUSHION FILLINGS AND INNERS

It is very easy to make your own inners for scatter cushions. This also provides a good opportunity to use up scrap calico or curtain lining. Various kinds of filling can be used. Whichever you choose, be sure to use a light colour for the inner and the filling – especially if the outer scatter cushion cover is to be cream or white, as indeed it will be if you're using calico.

I have found that the following materials generally make good filling for scatter cushion inners:

🌑 *Sponge chips* are relatively inexpensive and are usually quite easily obtainable. Ensure that the cushion inner is well filled – paying particular attention to the corners of square and rectangular cushions – as, in my experience, the foam chips tend to flatten a little after a few days' use. Nonetheless, this is the filling material I recommend and use most often myself.

🌑 *Polyester wadding* is sold by the metre or yard, or as scrap pieces by weight, and is also relatively inexpensive. Use offcuts or cut it into pieces no larger than about 20 cm x 20 cm (8 in x 8 in).

🌑 *Down* and *feathers* give a luxurious appearance and weighty feel. I recommend this filling for cushions that are in daily use in places like TV rooms, provided that nobody in the family is allergic to down!

MAKING A CUSHION INNER

To make a cushion inner, measure the outer cover and add a 1 cm (⅜ in) seam allowance all round. Cut two pieces of calico to these measurements. With right sides together, stitch the two pieces together all the way round, leaving an opening of about 15 cm (6 in) in a convenient place. Turn the work the right way out and fill the inner with your choice of filling, being sure to fill any corners carefully. Slipstitch neatly to close.

4. Stitch a piece of 14 mm-wide (½ in-wide) ribbon in each of the following four positions: from point A to G, point G to D, from point D to J, and from point J to point A (*see* Figure 2).

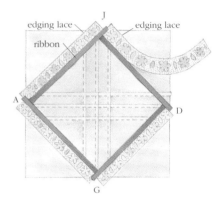

5. Stitch a piece of edging lace parallel to the outside edge of each ribbon strip, with edges just touching (*see* Figure 2). If you are using broderie anglaise, use satin ribbon to cover the raw edges.

6. For the frill, cut a strip of calico no more than 9 cm (3½ in) wide and double the perimeter of the scatter cushion. If necessary, join strips of calico using French seams (*see* Making a French Seam, page 8) to obtain the required length. Overlock or zigzag one long side of the frill. Gather the other long side (*see* Gathering a Frill, page 8) so that it fits around the perimeter of the cushion cover.

7. Place the frill and the decorated cover right sides together and pin the gathered edge of the frill around the perimeter of the cushion cover. Round the four corners slightly (*see* Figure 3). Stitch, leaving about 2.5 cm (1 in) loose at each end. Join the two loose ends of the frill using a French seam (*see* Making a French Seam, page 8) and complete stitching.

8. To make a cushion cover with an overlap opening at the back, cut two backing pieces of calico,

A lumpy filling can spoil the look of a beautiful cushion cover.

each measuring 42 cm x 30 cm
(16½ in x 12 in). Turn over a
double 1 cm (⅜ in) hem along
one 42 cm-side (16½ in-side) of
each backing piece.

9. With right sides together, pin
the cushion cover front, with the
frill folded towards the centre, and
one overlap together (*see* Figure 3).
Stitch from point A, through B and
C to point D to attach the overlap,
working 1 cm (⅜ in) from the
edge. Work carefully around the
two corners, making sure that you
don't catch the frill as you stitch.

FIGURE 3

10. Repeat this process with the
second backing piece, also right
side down. The two backing
pieces should overlap by about
15 cm (6 in) (*see* Figure 4).

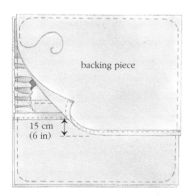

FIGURE 4

11. Cut away excess fabric around
the edges, and overlock or zigzag
all around. Turn the work right
side out and turn up a 1 cm (⅜ in)
hem along the edge of the frill.

Bolster-style Neck Cushions (page 37) offer an interesting shape variation.

33

ROUND SCATTER CUSHION COVER WITH LATTICE CENTRE

This unusual, round scatter cushion cover is definitely intended for decorative purposes only – on a bed or chaise longue, for example – and should not be used where it will be subjected to everyday wear and tear.

REQUIREMENTS

70 cm x 150 cm-wide (¾ yd x 59 in-wide) calico

6 m x 14 mm-wide (6½ yd x ½ in-wide) satin ribbon

matching cotton thread

2 m x 8 cm-wide (2½ yd x 3¼ in-wide) edging lace

3.5 m x 2.5 cm-wide (4 yd x 1 in-wide) edging lace

1. From the calico, cut out a square measuring 42 cm x 42 cm (16½ in x 16½ in), fold it in half, and in half again, and finger press. Referring to the instructions in Steps 3 and 4 on page 24, cut out a circle from this square; set aside.

2. Cut out a square of calico measuring 15 cm x 15 cm (6 in x 6 in) and cut about 20 strips of 14 mm-wide (½-in wide) satin ribbon, each 20 cm (8 in) in length. Starting about 2 cm (¾ in) from the top edge of the square, pin ten strips of the ribbon in horizontal rows, next to and

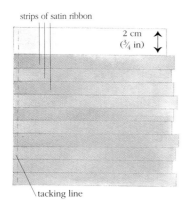

strips of satin ribbon

2 cm (¾ in)

tacking line

FIGURE 1A

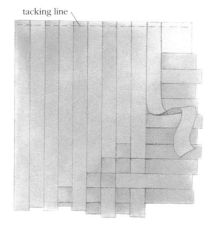

tacking line

FIGURE 1B

touching one another, to cover the square of calico. Very carefully, tack in place down the one side (*see* Figure 1a), then stitch down neatly and securely.

3. Working along the top edge of the square, repeat the procedure, arranging the remaining ten lengths of ribbon to form vertical rows over the horizontal rows, covering the 2 cm (¾ in) gap in the process (*see* Figure 1b). Along the top edge, tack the rows of ribbon carefully, then stitch them down securely. You should now have a small square of calico covered with rows of ribbon stitched down along two sides and lying across each other loosely.

4. The next step is to weave the vertical and horizontal rows of ribbon through each other (*see* photograph, page 32). Once the weaving is complete, carefully tack the two loose sides down and stitch carefully and securely. You should now have a square of calico, covered with a weaving of satin ribbon.

5. As you are making a round scatter cushion, the square weaving now needs to be cut to a circular shape. Using the same method as in Step 1, draw a

circular shape with a soft pencil on the square weaving. Tack and carefully stitch along this circular line, then cut the shape just outside this stitching line.

6. Returning to the circular piece of calico you cut out in Step 1, stitch your small woven ribbon circle down neatly in the centre of the larger circle. Cover the raw edge of the ribbon circle with a frill made of 8 cm-wide (3¼ in-wide) edging lace twice the circumference of the ribbon circle (*see* Gathering a Frill, page 8). With the right side up, pin the lace frill into place so that it overlaps the edge of the ribbon circle slightly, spreading the gathers evenly. Stitch down and join the ends of the lace neatly (*see* Joining Ribbon and Lace, page 9).

7. To make the frill for the cushion cover, cut a strip of calico about 9 cm (3½ in) wide, and double the circumference of the bigger circle. If necessary, join strips of calico using French seams (*see* Making a French Seam, page 8) to obtain the required length. Overlock or zigzag one long side of the frill. Gather the other long side (*see* Gathering a Frill, page 8) to fit the circumference of the cushion cover. Join the ends of the frill using a French seam (*see* Making a French Seam, page 8).

8. Position the frill, right side up, on the right side of the cushion cover, so that the gathered edge of the calico frill will be covered slightly by the lace frill (*see* Figure 2). Pin the calico frill into position and stitch down neatly and firmly, making sure that the gathers are spread evenly around the circumference. Stitch 14 mm-wide (½ in-wide) satin ribbon over the raw edge of the calico frill, using a row of small, straight stitches close to each edge of the ribbon. Secure the loose end of the ribbon neatly to finish (*see* Joining Ribbon and Lace, page 9).

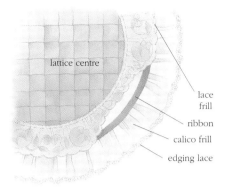

lattice centre

lace frill

ribbon

calico frill

edging lace

FIGURE 2

9. Stitch 2.5 cm-wide (1 in-wide) edging lace along the edge of the calico frill all round.

10. Make an overlap opening for the back of the cushion cover as described in Steps 8–10 on page 33, trimming off the excess fabric to make a circle once you have joined the front to the back sections. Overlock or zigzag the raw edge to neaten.

VARIATIONS

❦ If the ribbon lattice centre is not to your liking, simply use a few rows of pin tucks (*see* Making Pin Tucks, page 9) and lace stitched diagonally across the circle.

❦ Use a piece of pretty, wide lace to form the decorative, circular central section of the cushion cover and fill it with fragrant potpourri before completing stitching. (I usually use nylon lace for this variation, as I find it has a finer weave, which prevents little bits of potpourri from spilling out.)

❦ The ribbon lattice centre of the cushion can also look very pretty if you interweave satin ribbon in two different shades of the same colour or in two altogether different colours.

❦ Why not make a rather romantic heart-shaped cushion (*see* photograph, page 41) instead of a simpler round one?

This highly decorative Round Scatter Cushion Cover with Lattice Centre is frilly, feminine and a little frivolous.

PIPED CUSHION COVER

Piping gives a neat, crisp edge that outlines the cushion's shape, resulting in a tailored, finished appearance. Piping looks great in a contrasting colour that is repeated elsewhere in the room.

REQUIREMENTS

42 cm x 150 cm-wide (16½ in x 59 in-wide) calico
1.7 m (1⅞ yd) piping, in the colour of your choice (*see* Note)
matching cotton thread

NOTE   You can either make your own piping (*see* Making Piping, page 9) or buy piping in calico or any of a number of other fabrics. If you are making your own piping, you will obviously require more fabric than listed here.

1. Cut a 42 cm x 42 cm (16½ in x 16½ in) square of calico.

2. Working on the right side of the calico, lay piping around the edge of the square, with the rounded edge of the piping lying inside the seam line (about 1.5 cm [⅝ in] from the edge) and the raw edges of the piping about 5 mm (¼ in) from the raw edges of the calico top. Tack into place, clipping into the piping seam allowance at the corners (*see* Figure 1a). Never take the piping

into a corner at an acute angle; round the corners off generously instead. For round cushions, snip notches into the seam allowance all around (*see* Figure 1b).

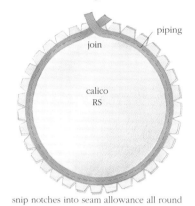

snip notches into seam allowance all round

FIGURE 1B

3. Join the end of the piping in the centre of one side, either butting the cord together or unravelling the threads and twisting them together, then folding under the piping fabric and overlapping the ends to neaten. Stitch the piping into position using the zipper or piping foot of your machine.

4. To make a cushion cover with an overlap opening at the back, cut two backing pieces of calico that each measure 42 cm x 30 cm (16½ in x 12 in). Turn over a double 1 cm (⅜ in) hem along one long side of each piece.

5. With right sides together, pin the front of your cushion cover and one overlap together. Attach the overlap using the special zipper or piping foot of your machine, using the piping stitching lines as a guide (work on the wrong side of the top of the cushion cover so that these stitches will be invisible).

6. Repeat this procedure with the second backing piece, also right side down. The two backing pieces should overlap by about 15 cm (6 in) (*see* Figure 4, page 33, for guidance).

7. Remove any bulkiness by trimming the seams to 5 mm (¼ in). Overlock or zigzag the raw edges and turn the cover right side out.

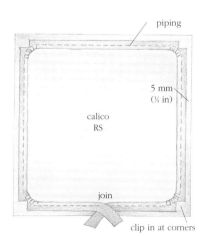

FIGURE 1A

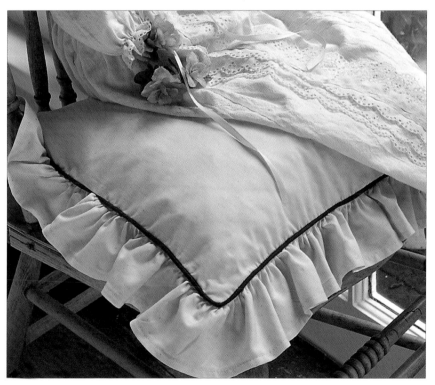

The contrast piping on this cushion cover is simple, yet elegant.

BOLSTER-STYLE NECK CUSHION

The bolster-style cushion – used mainly to offer neck support – can also be very pretty, creating an interesting shape variation in a pile of other scatter cushions on a bed .

REQUIREMENTS

37 cm x 150 cm-wide (14½ in x 59 in-wide) calico

2 m x 8 cm-wide (2⅛ yd x 3¼ in-wide) broderie anglaise or crochet lace

matching cotton thread

2 m x 2.5 cm-wide (2¼ yd x 1 in-wide) satin ribbon

50 cm x 8 mm-wide (20 in x ⅜ in-wide) satin ribbon

filling for bolster inner

1. Cut out a rectangle of calico measuring 50 cm x 37 cm (20 in x 14½ in).

2. Draw a soft pencil line 11 cm (4¼ in) in from each of the short ends (*see* Figure 1a). Cut the

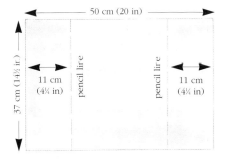

FIGURE 1A

length of lace in half (so that you have two pieces, each 1 m [40 in] long) and gather both pieces (*see* Gathering a Frill, page 8) to fit the width of the fabric. Pin the gathered lace into position on the pencil lines and stitch down, ensuring that the gathers are spread evenly (*see* Figure 1b).

3. Cover the raw edge of the lace with the 2.5 cm-wide (1 in-wide) satin ribbon (*see* Figure 1b), using

position lace and ribbon along this line

lace

ribbon

FIGURE 1B

a neat row of small stitches close to each edge of the ribbon.

4. With right sides together, join the raw edges of the calico together to form a tube. Overlock or zigzag to neaten the seam.

5. Turn back 1 cm (½ in) and then a further 1 cm (½ in) to form a casing about 1 cm (½ in) wide on each of the short sides. Finger press or press the casings using an iron. Stitch using a straight stitch, leaving an opening of about 2 cm (¾ in) before the side seam to allow you to thread the ribbon (*see* Figure 2a).

6. Thread 25 cm (10 in) of 8 mm-wide (⅜ in-wide) ribbon through each casing.

7. To make the bolster inner, cut a piece of calico measuring 39 cm x 36 cm (15¼ in x 14¼ in) and two circular end pieces, each with a diameter of 15 cm (6 in) (*see* Figure 2b). Join the two long sides of the rectangle to form a tube, right sides together, leaving an opening of 15 cm (6 in) in the centre of the seam. With right sides together, insert a circle of calico into each end of the tube. Working around the inside edge of each end of the tube, pin and stitch the circles into position.

8. Turn right side out, stuff with filling (*see* page 32), and hand stitch the opening closed.

9. Insert the inner into the bolster cushion, pull in the ribbons at each end to close, and tie the ribbons into bows.

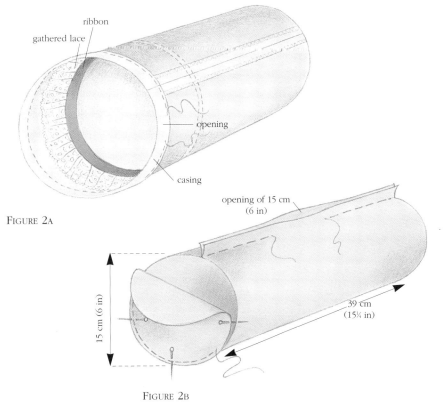

ribbon

gathered lace

opening

casing

FIGURE 2A

opening of 15 cm (6 in)

15 cm (6 in)

39 cm (15¼ in)

FIGURE 2B

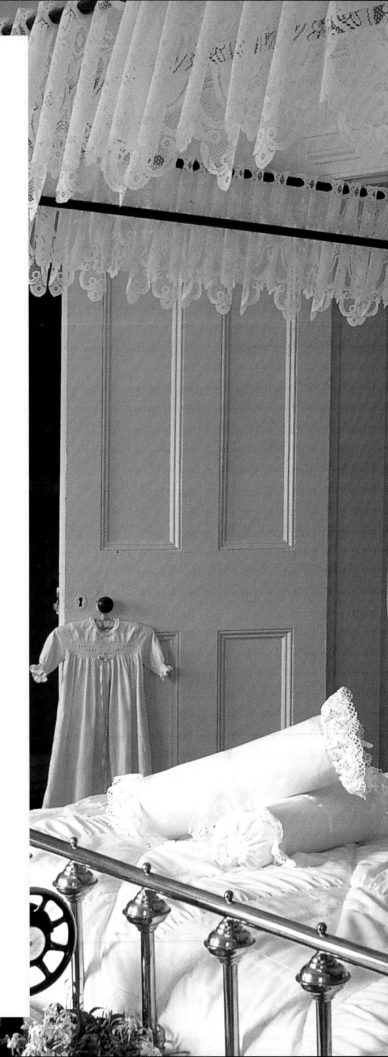

CHAPTER TWO

FOR THE
BEDROOM

*T*he bedroom is a private domain where
you retreat from daily pressures; the
decor should induce relaxation, allowing
you to feel refreshed at the start of each
new day. The bed forms the natural focal
point of the bedroom, and I suggest using
the duvet covering as a starting point
when deciding on the feel you'd like to
create. Bear in mind, though, that the
bed (especially a double bed) covers a
large amount of floor space. So, if you
choose a rather dominant bed covering, it
is likely that the eye will see little else.

DUVET COVERS

Anyone with a little knowledge and a sewing machine can make a simple duvet cover. Bear in mind, though, that as you spend roughly a third of your day tucked up under it, it might be worth your while spending some time creating something really special.

STANDARD DUVET SIZES

	WIDTH X LENGTH
Single	140 cm x 200 cm (55⅛ in x 78¾ in)
Double	200 cm x 200 cm (78 in x 78 in)
Queen	230 cm x 200 cm (not in the UK)
King	230 cm x 220 cm (90 in x 86 in)

If your particular duvet is not one of the standard sizes given above, measure its width and length and add 4 cm (1½ in) to each measurement (this includes 2 cm [¾ in] for hems and seam allowances, and 2 cm [¾ in] to allow for a good fit) to determine the size of the fabric you will need. Of course, this will exclude frill and flap requirements. The finished size of the cover will be the length and width measurements, with 2 cm (¾ in) added to each.

PIN TUCK AND LACE DUVET COVER

This duvet cover is made up of individual squares decorated with lace, ribbon and pin tucks that form an 'x' design. When the squares are joined, the design forms a symmetrical pattern that is pleasing to the eye.

The instructions given here are for making a duvet cover for a double bed, as this seems to be the most

REQUIREMENTS FOR PIN TUCK AND LACE DUVET COVER

DUVET SIZE	WIDTH (squares)	LENGTH (squares)	TOTAL
Single	2	4	8
Double	3	4	12
Queen (not UK)	4	4	16
King	4	4	16

popular size. The table above lists the number of squares required for duvets of other standard sizes. If your duvet is not a standard size, use the number of squares suggested for the size closest to yours, and adjust the width of the borders (see Steps 8–10) to achieve the desired finished width and length.

REQUIREMENTS
(Duvet for a double bed)

8.5 m x 150 cm-wide (9¼ yd x 59 in-wide)
calico
matching cotton thread
25 m x 14 mm-wide (27½ yd x ½ in-wide)
satin ribbon
25 m x 2.5 cm-wide (27½ yd x 1 in-wide)
edging lace (crochet lace or broderie anglaise)
8 m x 2.5 cm-wide (8¾ yd x 1 in-wide)
satin ribbon
8 m x 6 cm-wide (8¾ yd x 2¼ in-wide)
edging lace
4.2 m x 150 cm-wide (5 yd x 59 in-wide)
polycotton, for the backing
3–5 press studs or a few strips of Velcro for flap

1. Cut 12 squares of calico, each 48 cm x 48 cm (19 in x 19 in).

2. To determine the position of the first pin tuck, fold each square in half to form a triangle; press. Stitch a pin tuck along this fold, and another on each side of it, leaving a space of about 3 cm (1¼ in) between pin tucks (*see* Making Pin Tucks, page 9).

3. The second set of three pin tucks should cross the first set. To determine the position for the first of these pin tucks, fold the square

in half the other way to form a new triangle. Press as before, stitch the central pin tuck, and one on each side of it, again leaving a space of 3 cm (1¼ in) between pin tucks (*see* Figure 1).

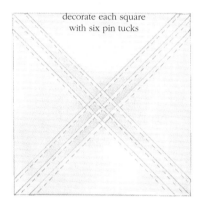

decorate each square with six pin tucks

FIGURE 1

4. Repeat this procedure to decorate each of the 12 squares with six pin tucks.

5. Measure 3 cm (1¼ in) outwards from each of the four outer pin tucks and draw a soft pencil line in these positions. Pin a length of 14 mm-wide (½ in-wide) ribbon along the outside of each of these lines, parallel to the appropriate rows of pin tucks. Stitch the ribbon down using a row of stitching close to each edge, unless you are using broderie anglaise. If you are using the latter, tuck the raw edge of the broderie anglaise under the outer edge of the ribbon before stitching it down. If you are using crochet lace, neatly stitch the lace down next to the ribbon (*see* Figure 2, page 41).

FIGURE 2

Pretty cushions complement the simplicity of this Easy Duvet Cover (page 44).

6. Using seams of 1 cm (⅜ in), join the squares to form four separate rows consisting of three squares each. Work very carefully when joining the squares to ensure that the patterns line up precisely (*see* photograph, page 42). If they do not line up, the overall design will not be symmetrical and the duvet cover will look untidy. Overlock or zigzag the raw edges.

7. When you have joined the squares to form four rows, join the rows, once again working meticulously to ensure that the squares line up correctly (*see* photograph, page 42). Overlock or zigzag the raw edges.

8. You have now completed the central part of the duvet cover, which consists of 12 decorated squares joined together. Next, you need to determine the width of the borders along the sides. Start by measuring the completed central part. As you want the finished cover to measure 202 cm x 202 cm (80 in x 80 in), or whatever the

case may be – you need to calculate how much fabric needs to be added to the length, and how much to the width.

9. To calculate the width of the top and bottom borders, subtract the length of the central part of the duvet cover from 202 cm (80 in), divide this measurement by two, and add 1 cm (⅜ in) to this measurement on each side for seam allowances. The length of each border should be the same as the width of the central part of the duvet cover.

10. To calculate the width of each side border, subtract the width of the central part of the duvet cover from 202 cm (80 in), divide this measurement by two, and add 1 cm to this measurement on each side for seam allowances. Calculate the length of the borders by adding the length of the central section to the width of the top and bottom borders, and add 2 cm (¾ in) for seam allowances.

11. Using a straight stitch, attach the top and bottom borders first, and then the side borders. Trim seams if necessary, then overlock or zigzag the raw edges to neaten.

12. Using the 2.5 cm-wide (1 in-wide) ribbon and lace, decorate all four of the borders. My borders are

Work meticulously when lining up the decorated squares.

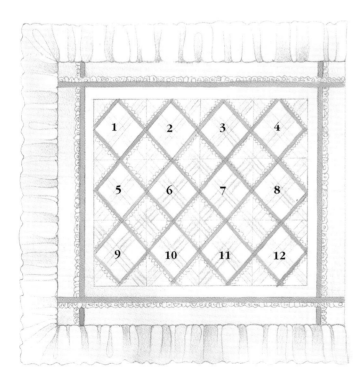

FIGURE 3

usually about 15 cm (6 in) wide, and I attach the ribbon in a line 5 cm (2 in) from the join with the central part, with the lace on the outer side. Allow the rows of ribbon and lace to cross at the corners (*see* Figure 3, below).

13. To make the frill, cut strips of calico 12 cm (4¾ in) wide to total 12 m (480 in/13 yds) in length when joined. I find the following formula useful when calculating how many strips to cut: as the frill needs to be sufficient for three sides of the duvet cover (2 x the length and 1 x the width), I add these measurements together. In this case this gives a total of 6 m (240 in/6½ yds). To allow for full gathers, I multiply this total by 2 (i.e. 6 m x 2 = 12 m [240 in x 2 = 480 in]). I now know that the strips need to total 12 m (480 in) in length when joined. As the calico I use is 150 cm (59 in) wide, I divide 12 m (480 in) by 150 cm (59 in, say 60 in), giving me an answer of 8. This means that I need eight strips of calico, each measuring 150 cm (60 in) in length.

14. Join the strips of calico using French seams (*see* Making a French Seam, page 8), and turn over a double 1 cm (⅜ in) hem along the two short sides of the long strip. Overlock or zigzag one long edge.

15. To gather the frill to fit along the three sides of the duvet cover, I suggest working with it in three sections of 4 m (160 in) each. It is easier to gather a length of 4 m (160 in) at a time, than to try to gather a frill as long as 12 m (13 yd). Before you begin gathering, use pins to mark off the frill into three 4 m-sections (160 in-sections). The position of the pins will indicate the position of the bottom corners of the duvet cover. Be sure to align the frill and the corners carefully, so that the frill is gathered evenly all round. Now gather each of the three sections that you have marked off along the raw edges (*see* Gathering a Frill, page 8).

16. Pin the gathered frill to the main section, right sides together, and stitch, rounding the corners slightly.

17. For the back of the duvet cover I recommend using polycotton, as most people find it more comfortable against their bodies than calico. As polycotton is usually only 1.5 m (59 in) wide, you will have to join it to obtain the required width. I recommend that you make a join down each side, rather than one in the centre. Begin by cutting two pieces of polycotton, each measuring 212 cm (87 in) in length. Set aside one piece, which will form the central section of the back.

18. Cut the second piece of polycotton lengthwise to obtain a strip measuring 54 cm x 212 cm (21½ in x 87 in). Fold this strip in half lengthwise and cut along the fold to obtain two narrower strips, each measuring 27 cm (10¾ in) in width. This means that you will have two 25 cm-wide (10 in-wide) strips, each with a 1 cm (⅜ in) seam allowance on either side.

19. Pin one of these strips to each of the relevant sides of the central backing piece (*see* Step 17), right sides together, and stitch to join (*see* Figure 4).

20. To make the bottom hem on the polycotton backing, which will be positioned at the opening of the duvet cover, fold 5 cm (2 in) and then a further 5 cm (2 in) to the wrong side, to form a double hem. Stitch down neatly.

21. To make a small flap to accommodate the Velcro strips or press studs, you will need a strip of calico 8 cm (3¼ in) wide and 202 cm (80 in) (i.e. the width of the duvet cover) in length.

22. Fold the strip in half lengthwise and overlock or zigzag the two long sides together. Position the strip along the bottom edge of the duvet cover on top of the frill, aligning the raw edge of the duvet cover with the overlocked edge of the strip. Straight stitch alongside the overlocking to attach.

23. To attach the polycotton backing piece to the front, place right sides together with the hemmed edge of the backing piece along the bottom edge (*see* Figure 5), and pin into position. Stitch together 30 cm (12 in) of the cover at one end of the bottom edge, work up the side, across the top, down the other side and 30 cm (12 in) inwards along the other end of the bottom edge, thereby leaving most of the bottom edge open. Trim, then neaten raw edges by overlocking or zigzagging.

backing piece
WS

RS

WS

flap for Velcro or press studs

FIGURE 5

24. Turn the work right side out. Turn a 1 cm (⅜ in) hem to the wrong side along the edge of the frill and stitch.

25. Attach several 5 cm-strips (2 in-strips) of Velcro to the opening flap, or use press studs.

VARIATIONS

❦ I find that using coloured ribbon on each of the squares tends to spoil the overall effect. The eye is drawn to the diamond shapes that are formed, and the other intricate details are lost. If you would like to use coloured ribbon, however, I suggest that you use it to decorate the side strips or borders of the duvet cover. This can look very pretty and introduce some colour.

❦ Make a double frill by gathering 8 cm-wide (3¼ in-wide) edging lace with the calico frill so that the lace lies on top of the calico.

❦ Stitch 2.5 cm-wide (1 in-wide) edging lace to the edge of the calico frill all round.

❦ Stitch the pin tucks to form a '+' shape, rather than an 'x' shape. Position the ribbon to form a diamond, using the centre points of each of the sides of the squares as your 'corners'.

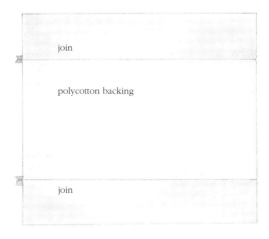

join

polycotton backing

join

FIGURE 4

EASY DUVET COVER

This duvet cover is beautiful and feminine, but quite simple (see photograph, page 41) and straightforward to make.

REQUIREMENTS
(Duvet for a double bed)

4.04 m x 150 cm-wide (4½ yd x 59 in-wide) calico
matching cotton thread
4.1 m x 2.5 cm-wide (4½ yd x 1 in-wide) satin ribbon
8.2 m x 2.5 cm-wide (9 yd x 1 in-wide) edging lace
4.4 m x 150 cm-wide (5 yd x 59 in-wide) polycotton, for the backing
3–5 press studs or a few strips of Velcro for flap

1. As calico is usually only 150 cm (59 in) wide, you will have to join the fabric to obtain the required width. I recommend making a join down each side, rather than a join in the centre. Begin by cutting two pieces of calico, each measuring 202 cm (80 in) in length. Set aside one piece, which will form the central front section.

2. Cut the second piece of calico lengthwise to obtain a strip measuring 54 cm x 202 cm (21½ in x 80 in). Fold this strip in half lengthwise and cut along the fold to obtain two narrower strips, each 27 cm (10¾ in) in width. This means that you will have two 25 cm-wide (10 in-wide) strips, each with a 1 cm (⅜ in) seam allowance on either side.

3. With right sides together, pin a strip to each of the relevant sides of the central front piece; stitch to join. Overlock or zigzag raw edges.

4. Working on the right side, position a length of 2.5 cm-wide (1 in-wide) satin ribbon over each of the two joins (*see* Figure 1). Pin and stitch down neatly, using a row of stitching close to each edge of the ribbon.

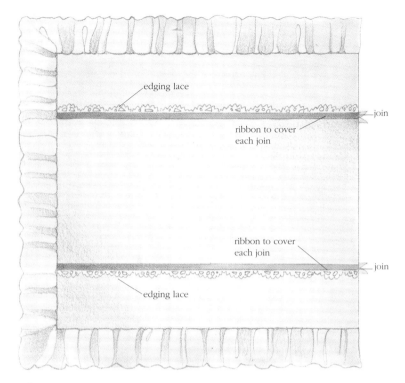

FIGURE 1

(labels on figure: edging lace · ribbon to cover each join · join · ribbon to cover each join · join · edging lace)

5. Pin the 2.5 cm-wide (1 in-wide) edging lace into position along the outside of the ribbon on each side (*see* Figure 1). Stitch down along the side closest to the ribbon.

6. To make the frill, cut eight strips of calico, each measuring 150 cm (59 in) in length and 12 cm (4¾ in) in width. Join these strips using French seams (*see* Making a French Seam, page 8) to give you a frill measuring approximately 12 m (13 yd). Overlock or zigzag one long side and hem the two short sides of the frill. Gather the frill (*see* Gathering a Frill, page 8), and with right sides together, pin into position and attach to the three sides, following Steps 15 and 16 of the Pin Tuck and Lace Duvet Cover on pages 42–43.

7. Using the polycotton, make the back of the duvet cover, following Steps 17–20 of the Pin Tuck and Lace Duvet Cover on page 43.

8. Make the flap for the bottom edge, following Steps 21–22 of the Pin Tuck and Lace Duvet Cover on page 43.

9. With the right sides together, attach the polycotton backing piece to the front of the duvet cover, following the instructions in Step 23 of the Pin Tuck and Lace Duvet Cover on page 43.

10. Turn the duvet cover right side out. Turn over a 1 cm (⅜ in) hem along the edge of the frill and stitch.

11. Attach 5 cm-strips (2 in-strips) of Velcro or press studs to the inside edges of the flap.

VARIATIONS
❧ Use 2.5 cm-wide (1 in-wide) satin ribbon in a contrasting colour to cover the joins. Choose a shade or colour that will blend in with the decor of the room.

❧ Stitch 2.5 cm-wide (1 in-wide) edging lace to the edge of the calico frill all round.

❧ Omit the ribbon and lace and insert piping between the central panel and the side sections and between the main section and the frill (*see* Making Piping, page 9).

FRILLED PILLOWCASE

*If you have taken the time
and made the effort to dress your
bed with a beautiful, handmade
duvet cover, it would be a real pity
not to complete the look by adding
these matching pillowcases, which
are relatively simple to make.
For a plainer, but very elegant
effect, omit the frill.*

REQUIREMENTS

(Standard pillow measuring approximately
70 cm x 40 cm [27½ in x 15¾ in])

88 cm x 150 cm-wide (34¾ in x 59-in wide)
calico
matching cotton thread
2.5 m x 14 mm-wide (2¾ yd x ½ in-wide)
satin ribbon
2.5 m x 2.5 cm-wide (2¾ yd x 1 in-wide)
edging lace

This Frilled Pillowcase has been decorated diagonally from corner to corner.

1. Cut a rectangular piece of calico measuring 43 cm x 72 cm (17 in x 28½ in) for the front of the pillowcase.

2. Starting about 3 cm (1¼ in) from the edge, make two parallel pin tucks, 3 cm (1¼ in) apart, along one short side of the rectangle (*see* Making Pin Tucks, page 9). Repeat along the remaining three sides (*see* Figure 1). Press the pin tucks so that they all lie in the same direction (either inwards or outwards).

3. Measure 3 cm (1¼ in) inwards from each of the inner pin tucks and draw soft pencil lines in these positions. Pin satin ribbon along these four lines (*see* Figure 1) and stitch down with a row of stitches close to each edge of the ribbon.

4. Pin a length of 2.5 cm-wide (1 in-wide) lace alongside each of the four lengths of ribbon, with the straight edge of the lace touching the inner edge of the ribbon (*see* Figure 1). Stitch the straight edge of the lace down neatly, leaving the scalloped edge free.

5. To make the frill, cut strips of calico 9 cm (3½ in) wide to total 4.5 m (5 yd) in length when joined. Join the strips to make a long strip, using French seams (*see* Making a French Seam, page 8).

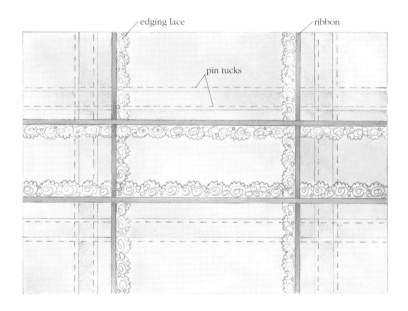

edging lace

ribbon

pin tucks

FIGURE 1

45

Gather the frill (*see* Gathering a Frill, page 8) to fit the rectangle. With the right sides of the frill and the rectangle together, pin the frill into position and stitch down all round. Overlock or zigzag the free edge of the frill.

6. For the back of the pillowcase, cut a piece of calico measuring 73 cm x 45 cm (28¾ in x 17¾ in), and a flap measuring 45 cm x 17 cm (17¾ in x 6¾ in). Hem one 45 cm-side (17¾ in-side) of each of these pieces.

7. Place the large backing piece on top of the front piece, right sides together. Position the hemmed edge of the backing piece so that it lies 2 cm (¾ in) short of the stitching line for the frill (*see* Figure 2 of the Continental Pillowcase, page 47). Pin the two pieces together on three sides, leaving the hemmed edge open.

8. Place the flap section right side down on top of the backing piece. Pin into position along three sides, leaving the hemmed edge open (*see* Figure 3 of the Continental Pillowcase, page 47).

9. Finally, neatly stitch the two backing pieces to the front piece all round. Zigzag or overlock the raw edges and turn the work right side out. Turn a 1 cm (⅜ in) hem to the wrong side along the bottom of the frill and neatly stitch down all round.

VARIATIONS
❧ This pillowcase can be made to match the Continental Pillowcase on page 47 (*see* photograph below).

❧ Instead of using lace and ribbon, simply use neat and elegant piping in a contrasting colour between the main section of the pillowcase and the frill.

❧ Stitch 2.5 cm-wide (1 in-wide) edging lace along the edge of the frill all the way round.

These relatively simple Continental Pillowcases (page 47) create a warm and inviting atmosphere.

CONTINENTAL PILLOWCASE

I feel that any bed without two Continental pillows on it looks unfinished. Most people I know don't use the Continental pillows when sleeping, but they make great back rests when you're lying in bed reading, or sitting up doing the crossword. During the day they offer a solid base for a pile of more decorative scatter cushions.

REQUIREMENTS

1.65 m x 150 cm-wide (1¾ yd x 59 in-wide) calico
matching cotton thread
1.2 m x 2.5 cm-wide (1¼ yd x 1 in-wide) satin ribbon
2.4 m x 6 cm-wide (2¾ yd x 2¼ in-wide) crochet lace
Velcro or press studs (optional)

1. Cut out a square piece of calico measuring 82 cm x 82 cm (32¼ in x 32¼ in).

2. Working diagonally from corner to corner across the centre of the square (*see* Figure 1), pin the satin ribbon to the calico. Stitch down neatly with a row of stitches close to each edge of the ribbon.

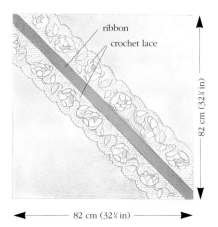

FIGURE 1

3. Pin a strip of crochet lace along each side of the ribbon (*see* Figure 1) and stitch down neatly.

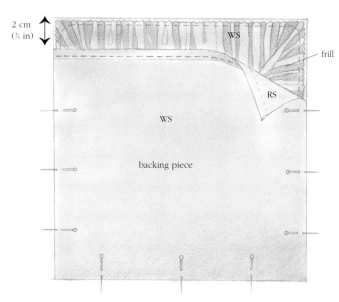

FIGURE 2

4. To make the frill, cut strips of calico 9 cm (3½ in) wide to total 6 m (6½ yd) in length when joined. Using French seams (*see* Making a French Seam, page 8) join all the strips to form a circle. Gather the frill (*see* Gathering a Frill, page 8) to fit the pillow. With the right sides of the gathered frill and the decorated square together, pin the frill into position along the gathered edge. Stitch the frill down carefully, taking care to round the corners slightly. Swing your work round and tuck the frill back as you go to avoid catching it in the line of stitching

5. Trim away any bulkiness and neaten the raw edges. Overlock or zigzag the free edge of the frill, turn a 1 cm (⅜ in) hem to the wrong side, and neatly stitch down all round.

6. To make the back of the pillowcase, cut a piece of calico measuring 83 cm x 83 cm (32¾ in x 32¾ in) and a piece of calico measuring 83 cm x 25 cm (32¾ in x 10 in). Hem one 83 cm-side (32¾ in-side) of each piece of calico by turning 1 cm (⅜ in) and then a further 1 cm (⅜ in) to the wrong side and stitching.

7. Place the square backing piece on top of the decorated calico

square, right sides together. Position the hemmed edge of the backing piece so that it lies 2 cm (¾ in) short of the stitching line for the frill (*see* Figure 2). Pin the two pieces together on three sides, leaving the hemmed edge open.

8. Now place the flap section right side down on top of the square backing piece, aligning raw edges as shown in Figure 3. Pin into position along three sides, again leaving the hemmed edge open.

9. Finally, stitch the two backing pieces to the front piece all around. Zigzag or overlock the raw edges and turn the work to the right side.

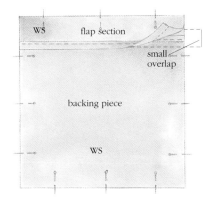

FIGURE 3

10. If necessary, attach Velcro or three press studs to the opening of the pillowcase.

VARIATIONS

❦ To make a slightly more fancy pillowcase, stitch some 2.5 cm-wide (1 in-wide) edging lace to the edge of the frill all round.

❦ Instead of using lace and ribbon, simply use piping in a contrasting colour between the main section and the frill.

❦ Decorate the front of the pillowcase using several rows of narrow pin tucks (*see* Making Pin Tucks, page 9).

❦ Use rows of ribbon and lace in different ways. Instead of working diagonally from corner to corner, work in lines parallel to the sides of the pillowcase, or allow the lines to cross in the centre.

NIGHT FRILLS

A night frill or valance generally serves to hide the base of a bed and create a neat, finished appearance. Some people like to use the same fabric as for the duvet, quilt or bedspread; others prefer introducing another colour, which can be repeated elsewhere in the room. If you have a beautiful brass bed, consider having no night frill at all – unless you need some hidden storage space under the bed! If you have a bed with posts or an upright frame at the foot, you will need to split the night frill at the bottom corners (see Making a Night Frill with Split Corners, page 49, and the photograph below). The amount of fabric required will depend on the size of your mattress base. The chart below offers a guide to standard mattress sizes.

STANDARD MATTRESS SIZES		
	LENGTH	WIDTH
Single	190 cm (6 ft 4 in)	92 cm (3 ft)
Double	190 cm (6 ft 4 in)	150 cm (4 ft 6 in)
King	190 cm (6 ft 4 in)	153 cm (5 ft)

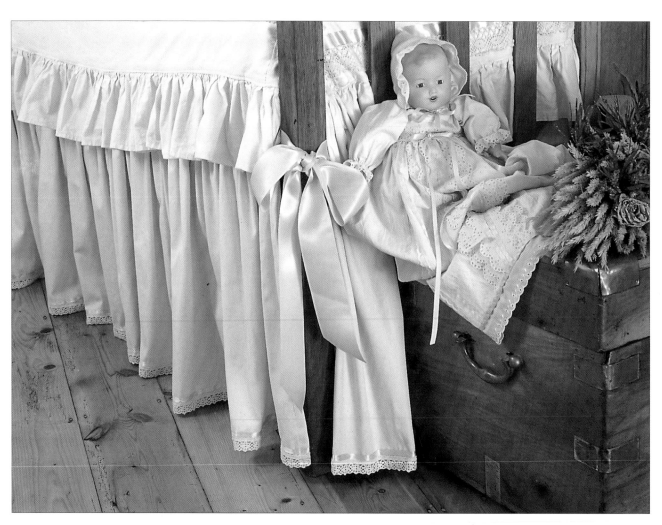

A pretty Night Frill with Split Corners (page 49) accommodates the lovely wooden frame of this bed.

GATHERED NIGHT FRILL

This is a good choice if you want to create a feminine or cottagey look. The amount of fabric required will vary depending on a number of different factors. One needs to bear in mind the height, size and design of the bed, the height of the particular mattress base or possible absence thereof, and so on. No particular size has been specified here, but the instructions will enable you to make a night frill to suit your needs.

REQUIREMENTS

polycotton for the central section (amount will depend on size of bed; *see* Step 1, below)
matching cotton thread
calico for the frill (amount will depend on size of bed; *see* Steps 4–6, below)

1. Begin by making the central section of the night frill (the part that will lie under the mattress) from polycotton. Measure the length and width of the bed, and add 3 cm (1¼ in) to the length measurement and 2 cm (¾ in) to the width measurement for hems and seam allowances.

2. If the polycotton you are using for this section is narrower than the width of the mattress, you will need to make joins. I suggest using a full width of polycotton down the centre, with narrower strips of equal width added on to each side to obtain the required width.

3. Once the central section is complete, round the bottom two corners slightly to fit the shape of the bed, if necessary. Hem the top edge by turning 1 cm (⅜ in) and then a further 1 cm (⅜ in) to the wrong side, and stitching.

4. You now need to calculate the amount of calico needed for the frill. Begin by measuring the distance between the top of the base of the bed and the floor (*see* Figure 1). Add 2 cm (¾ in) to this measurement for seam allowances. This will give you the width (drop) of the frill.

5. As the frill will need to fit around three sides of the bed as well as a little of the top end, multiply the length of the bed by 2, and add this measurement to the width of the bed. To allow sufficient fabric for gathering, multiply this total by 2, i.e. [(length of bed x 2) + width of bed] x 2 = total length of frill.

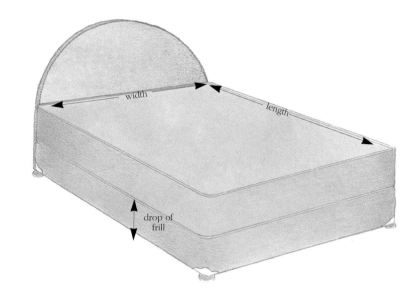

FIGURE 1

MAKING A NIGHT FRILL WITH SPLIT CORNERS

If there is an upright frame at the foot of the bed it will be necessary to make the frill in three separate sections. Prepare two strips of calico measuring twice the length of the bed, and one measuring twice the width of the base. If necessary, join strips to obtain the required length using French seams (*see* Making a French Seam, page 8). Make a hem

FIGURE 1

at both short ends of each strip by turning 1 cm (⅜ in) and then a further 1 cm (⅜ in) to the wrong side. Gather the strips to fit the relevant sections (*see* Gathering a Frill, page 8), making sure that 1.5 cm (⅜ in) will be left clear on either side of the two bottom corners. Join the strips to the main section, using Steps 9–11 on page 50 as a guide.

6. To determine how many strips of calico you need to cut, divide the total length of the frill by the width of the calico (150 cm [59 in]). To determine the total amount of calico you require, multiply the number of strips by the total width of the frill (including the 2 cm [¾ in] seam allowance).

7. Join the strips using French seams (*see* Making a French Seam, page 8), and turn over a double 1 cm (⅜ in) hem to the wrong side on each short side of the frill.

8. Use pins along the top edge to divide the frill into six equal sections along its length. Gather each of the sections separately, as this is much easier than trying to gather the frill in its entirety (*see* Gathering a Frill, page 8).

9. To ensure that the frill will be positioned correctly and gathered evenly all round, mark off six points around the perimeter of the central section, starting and ending 15 cm (6 in) from the corners along the top edge. To calculate the distance between points, multiply the length of the bed by two, add the width, plus 30 cm (12 in), and divide this total by 6.

10. The frill is attached to three sides of the central section, extending only about 15 cm (6 in) along each side of the top end (*see* Figure 2). With the right sides of the central section and the frill together, pin the frill into position

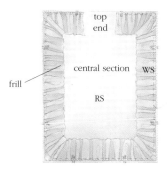

FIGURE 2

all round, carefully aligning the six points you have marked off on the central section with the six points along the frill.

11. Stitch the frill down all round, and then overlock or zigzag the raw edges of the seam. On the right side, topstitch 5 mm (¼ in) from the seamline so that the seam is stitched down flat, lying towards the centre of the bed.

12. Overlock or zigzag the bottom edge of the frill and turn under a 1 cm (⅜ in) hem.

VARIATIONS

❦ Decorate the bottom edge of the frill with satin ribbon and lace.

❦ If your sewing machine offers decorative stitches, use rows of stitching in contrasting colours along the bottom edge of the frill.

❦ A night frill with a scalloped edge is very attractive. Some sewing machines have special attachments that make this relatively easy to accomplish.

❦ Edge the night frill with bias binding in a contrasting colour.

FITTED NIGHT FRILL
WITH INVERTED PLEATS

This tailored night frill is unfussy and suited to a fairly masculine decorating style. It fits neatly and includes an inverted pleat at each of the bottom corners. A fitted bedspread and a large bolster cushion along the top of the bed complement the design well.

REQUIREMENTS

polycotton for the central section (amount will depend on size of bed; *see* Step 1, below)
matching cotton thread
calico for the frill (amount will depend on size of bed; *see* Steps 4–6, below)

1. Begin by making the central section of the night frill (the part that will lie under the mattress) from polycotton. Measure the length and width of the bed base, and add 3 cm (1¼ in) to the length measurement and 2 cm (¾ in) to the width measurement for seam allowances and hems.

2. If the polycotton you are using for this section is narrower than the width of the mattress, you will need to make joins. I suggest using a full width of polycotton down the centre, with narrower strips of equal width attached to each side to obtain the required width.

3. Once the central section is complete, round the bottom two corners slightly to fit the shape of the base, if necessary, and hem the top edge by turning back 1 cm (¾ in) and a further 1 cm (¾ in).

4. You now need to calculate the amount of calico needed for the frill. Begin by measuring the distance between the top of the base of the bed and the floor (*see* Figure 1, page 49). Add 2 cm (1½ in) to this measurement for seam allowances. This will give you the width (drop) of the frill.

5. As the frill will need to fit around three sides of the bed, multiply the length of the bed by two, and add this measurement to the width of the bed. Add on 80 cm (31½ in) for each of the two inverted pleats. This is the total amount of fabric required for the length of the night frill. It will be best to buy this amount of fabric rather than to join strips, as the joins will be visible.

6. If, however, you need to join strips of calico, determine how many strips you need to cut, by dividing the total length of the frill in cm (in/yds) by 150 (59) (calico is usually 150 cm [59 in] wide). To determine the total amount of

50

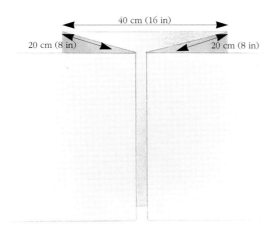

40 cm (16 in)

20 cm (8 in)   20 cm (8 in)

FIGURE 1

all round, carefully making an inverted pleat, 20 cm [8 in] deep, (*see* Figure 1) at each of the bottom corners.

9. Stitch the frill down all round, and then overlock or zigzag the raw edges of the seam. On the right side, topstitch 5 mm (¼ in) from the seamline so that the seam is stitched down flat, lying towards the centre of the bed.

10. Overlock or zigzag the bottom edge of the frill to neaten, then turn a 1 cm (⅜ in) hem to the wrong side. Stitch into place.

fabric required, multiply the number of strips by the total width of the frill (including the 2 cm [¾ in] seam allowance).

7. Join the strips of calico for the frill using French seams (*see* Making a French Seam, page 8).

Try to position the joins so that they will fall on the inside of the inverted pleats. Hem the two short ends of the frill.

8. With the right sides of the central section and the frill together, pin the frill into position

VARIATIONS

❧ For an elegant finish, attach bias binding to the bottom edge of the night frill.

❧ Stitch a length of ribbon all the way along the frill 5 cm (2 in) from the bottom edge.

A Fitted Night Frill with Inverted Pleats (page 50) is unfussy and neat.

FITTED BEDSPREAD

*Many people seem to regard a
fitted bedspread as something rather
old-fashioned and outdated,
but I still receive a surprising number
of requests for this kind of bed
covering. To my mind, a fitted
bedspread is most suitable for a guest
room, where the bed is seldom used
and is usually covered by only
a bottom sheet, while blankets
are stored elsewhere.
The fitted bedspread looks good
with a gathered frill, or one that
has straight sides and inverted pleats
at the bottom corners. This style of
bed cover is not suitable for a bed
with an upright metal or wooden
frame, because the split corners
will be too noticeable.*

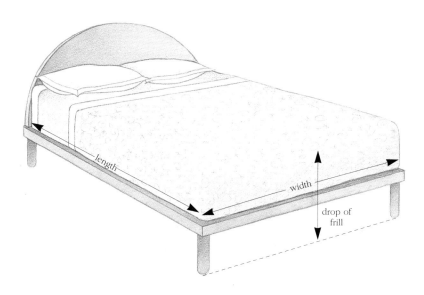

FIGURE 1

REQUIREMENTS

calico (*see* Steps 1–3 and 9–10, below)
matching cotton thread
compressed wadding (*see* Step 4, below)
14 mm-wide (½ in-wide) satin ribbon
2.5 cm-wide (1 in-wide) edging lace
10 cm-wide (4 in-wide) edging lace

1. As this bedspread is designed
to fit quite snugly, you will need to
decide what kind of bedclothes are
likely to be used underneath. It is
best to make the bed, using the
sheets and blankets you would
normally use, before taking the
measurements. Then measure the
length and the width of the top of
the bed, across all the bedclothes
(*see* Figure 1). Add a seam allowance
of 1.5 cm (⅝ in) all round.

2. To calculate the width (drop) of
the frill, measure from the top of
the bed (including the bedclothes)
to the floor (*see* Figure 1), and add
a seam allowance of 2.5 cm (1 in)
to this measurement.

3. Begin by cutting out the central
section of the bedspread, using the
measurements you obtained in
Step 1. As calico is usually only
150 cm (59 in) wide, you will

probably have to join sections
to obtain the required width. I
recommend using a full width
down the centre, and adding two
narrower strips of equal width
down the sides. Once you have
stitched this section together,
round the bottom corners slightly
to fit the shape of the mattress.

4. The next step entails cutting out
and stitching the wadding to form
a second central section. The
wadding should measure 1 cm
(⅜ in) wider all round than the
central calico section. If necessary,
join sections of wadding to obtain
the desired width. Position the
sections with their right sides
together, and make a narrow seam
using a straight stitch.

5. Place the wrong sides of the
calico and the wadding together,
and pin together carefully,
positioning the pins fairly close
together to ensure accuracy. Now
decide on the pattern you would
like to create when quilting, and
mark out lines along the calico
with a soft pencil. Tack along each
line. I find that a crisscross design
works well (*see* Figure 2), or
simple lines running parallel to

one another. Always start in the
centre when quilting, and work
outwards, leaving 15–20 cm
(6–8 in) between lines (*see* Figure 2).

6. Use satin ribbon and lace to
decorate the top of the quilted
section. Refer to the photograph
on the next page for ideas, or
create your own unique design.

7. Overlock or zigzag the top edge
of the quilted section (i.e. the pillow
end) and turn under a 1 cm (⅜ in)
hem. Stitch down neatly.

8. To make it easier to position the
frill correctly along the three sides
of the central section, mark off six
points, equal distances apart on
the central section. To determine
the distance between points,
multiply the length of the bed by

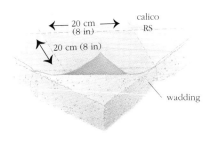

FIGURE 2

A simple Fitted Bedspread with a gathered frill is ideal for a pretty guest room, where the bed is seldom used.

two, and add the width. Divide this total by six and mark the points with pins.

9. Use the total you calculated in the previous step, i.e. (length x 2) + width, multiplied by two, to determine the total length of the frill required. (You multiply by two to allow for gathering.)

10. To determine how many strips of calico you need to cut, divide this total length in cm (in) by 150 (59) (calico is usually 150 cm [59 in] wide). To determine the total amount of fabric required for the frill, multiply the number of strips by the full width of the frill (including the 2.5 cm [1 in] seam allowance).

11. Cut the required number of strips and join together, using French seams (*see* Making a French Seam, page 8). Hem the two short ends of the frill.

12. You now need to mark off six points, equal distances apart, along the length of the frill. These points will correspond with the six points you marked off along the perimeter of the central section in Step 8. To determine the distance between points, divide the total length of the frill by six. Mark off these points with pins, and gather the frill to fit the two long sides and the width of the central section. It may be easier to gather each of the six sections of the frill individually before positioning.

13. With right sides together, pin the frill to the central section, lining up the marked points all round. Stitch down securely.

14. Overlock or zigzag the raw edges of the seam, and topstitch so that the seam lies flat, facing towards the centre of the bed.

15. Overlock or zigzag the bottom edge of the frill and turn under a hem of 1 cm (¾ in) to the wrong side. Decorate the edge of the frill with rows of ribbon and lace.

VARIATION

❧ Insert piping in a contrasting colour between the central section and the frill, and use matching bias binding along the bottom edge.

Make the most of a bed with beautiful cushions and a Comforter with Decorated Squares and Ruched Panels (page 55).

COMFORTERS

A comforter is a luxurious, but homely, warm quilt that can add a special ambience to an otherwise very simply decorated bedroom. Making a comforter is a real labour of love that may require a considerable amount of time and effort, but you will be rewarded with something valuable and quite unique. I suggest that you begin by making a small comforter for a baby's cot. Once you have mastered this size and had your confidence boosted by the beautiful end result, I'm sure you'll be inspired to try making a comforter for your own bed or for someone special.

Bear the following points in mind before attempting a comforter:

❀ *Always choose fabric that has been preshrunk and one that does not crease easily. Once completed, a comforter should only be very lightly pressed.*

❀ *Work extremely carefully and accurately when cutting and stitching, as edges and stitched lines need to be perfectly straight.*

❀ *Remember to use the same seam allowance throughout, to ensure that the various sections align properly.*

❀ *When preparing the top of the comforter, press each completed section before you attach the wadding and join it to other sections.*

❀ *When choosing the design of the comforter, consider using decorated squares which, when lined up in rows, create a pleasing overall effect.*

❀ *Always start quilting from the centre of the comforter. A domestic sewing machine may be used, but this is no easy task. Quilting this way requires a considerable amount of patience and arm muscle, but don't despair – the end result is well worth it!*

COMFORTER WITH DECORATED SQUARES AND RUCHED PANELS

This very special quilt is a challenging project that should not be tackled by beginners! I have suggested using lace to decorate the squares, but candlewicked squares also look particularly pretty.

REQUIREMENTS

(Comforter for a double bed)

10 m x 150 cm-wide (11 yd x 59 in-wide) calico
6 m x 150 cm-wide (6½ yd x 59 in-wide) polycotton, for the back
40 m x 2.5 cm-wide (44 yd x 1 in-wide) crochet lace
10 m x 8 cm-wide (11 yd x 3¼ in-wide) crochet lace
5 m x 2 m-wide (5½ yd x 80 in-wide) 200 g (very thick) wadding
matching cotton thread

1. Referring to Figure 1, cut 20 calico squares, each measuring 40 cm x 40 cm (15¾ in x 15¾ in). Cut 12 squares, 16 cm x 16 cm (6¼ in x 6¼ in) each. Cut 31 strips, each measuring 80 cm x 16 cm (31½ in x 6¼ in). If necessary, join sections to obtain the desired length using French seams (*see* Making a French Seam, page 8).

2. Decorate each square with 2.5 cm-wide (1 in-wide) crochet lace (*see* Figure 2).

crochet lace

FIGURE 2

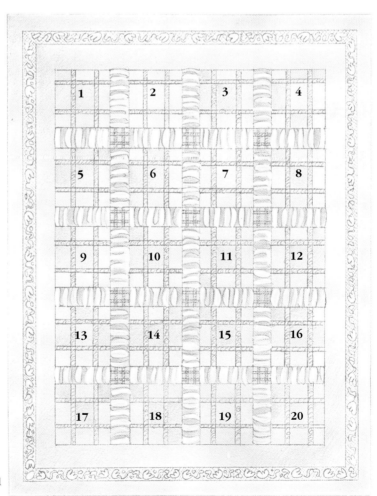

FIGURE 1

3. Gather each 80 cm x 16 cm (31½ in x 6¼ in) strip along both long sides, to a finished length of 40 cm (15¾ in).

4. With right sides together, join the long side of a ruched strip to one side of a decorated square. Repeat, alternating squares and ruched strips, until you have completed one horizontal row (*see* Figure 3). Overlock or zigzag the raw edges. Complete five horizontal rows, each consisting of four 40 cm x 40 cm (15¾ in x 15¾ in) squares and three ruched strips.

5. To create the panels between the rows, join a short side of a ruched strip to one side of a 16 cm x 16 cm (6¼ in x 6¼ in) square (*see* Figure 4). Repeat until you have four panels, each consisting of four ruched strips and three 16 cm x 16 cm (6¼ in x 6¼ in) squares.

6. Assemble the main section of the comforter by joining the horizontal rows of squares together, with a narrow panel between rows. For accuracy, first pin the sections together, with right sides together, making quite sure that all the seams line up. Stitch, then overlock or zigzag raw edges.

7. Measure the length of the main section; subtract this from the desired finished length, which in

FIGURE 3

this case will be 270 cm (106 in) (280 cm [110 in] less 10 cm [4 in] for the frill along the bottom edge). Divide your answer by 2, and add 2 cm (¾ in) for seam allowances; this will give you the width of the top and bottom borders. Cut out two strips of this width, measuring the same as the width of the main section in length.

8. To determine the width of the borders on the sides, measure the width of the main section and subtract this from the desired finished width, which in this case will be 215 cm (84½ in) (235 cm [92½ in] less 20 cm [8 in] for the frill on either side). Divide your answer by 2, and add 2 cm (¾ in) for seam allowances; this will give you the width of the two side borders. To determine the length of these borders, add the width of the top and bottom borders to the length of the main section. Cut out these two borders.

9. With right sides together, stitch the top and bottom borders and then the side borders to the main section. Decorate the borders with 8 cm-wide (3¼ in-wide) crochet lace running down the centre of each border and meeting at the corners (*see* Figure 1, page 55).

10. The strips for the frill will be 12 cm (4¾ in) wide. To calculate how many 150 cm (59 in) strips

you need, use the following formula: [width of comforter + (2 x length)] x 2 (to allow for gathering), divided by 150 cm (59 in). Join the strips for the frill together using French seams (*see* Making a French Seam, page 8). Overlock or zigzag one long side of the frill and make a 1 cm (⅜ in) hem. Gather the other side of the frill to fit around the perimeter of the quilt (*see* Gathering a Frill, page 8). Then set the frill aside.

11. Now you will need a piece of wadding that is 5 cm (2 in) longer than the comforter on all four sides. If the wadding you are using is not wide enough, make a join by aligning the edges of the two pieces and using a neat herring-bone stitch. Do not overlap the two pieces of wadding, as this will result in a bulky join. Turn the wadding over and reinforce the join by repeating the herringbone stitch on the other side.

12. Clear a fairly large area of floor space, lay the wadding on the carpet, and position the top of the quilt, right side up, on top of the wadding, smoothing it out.

13. Starting in the centre of the quilt, tack the top to the wadding using a long needle and medium-sized tacking stitches. You can tack in diagonal lines across the quilt, or in parallel lines. Smooth your work away from the centre after completing each line of tacking. The gap between the lines of tacking stitches should not be more than 30–40 cm (12–15¾ in).

14. Now comes the tricky part! The best way to work is to start in the centre, with the right-hand side of the comforter rolled up towards the centre and positioned under the arm of the machine (*see* Figure 5, page 57). Stitch along the tacking lines, working towards the right and unrolling the comforter as you go. Then swing

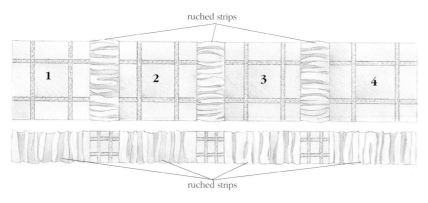

ruched strips

ruched strips

FIGURE 4

FIGURE 5

your work around, and again working from the centre, stitch the left-hand side in the same way.

15. Sew slowly and take breaks if necessary when you become tired! Do not pull or push the fabric while you are sewing, or the quilt will pucker. When working on the left-hand side, smooth the fabric outwards between the lines to prevent bulging.

16. Using a circular side plate or dinner plate, draw an arc on each of the bottom corners of the comforter, and trim away the excess fabric. Divide the perimeter of the comforter and the length of the frill into six equal sections each, using pins. Then, with right sides together, pin the frill into position, matching up each of the sections. (Remember that no frill is needed at the top of the quilt.) Stitch the frill down neatly and securely all the way round.

17. Measure the finished length and width of the quilt, excluding the frill, and cut the lining to this size, adding a 2 cm (¾ in) seam allowance on all four sides.

18. Place the lining and quilt right sides together and stitch together on the wrong side using the stitching line for the frill as your guide. Leave an opening of about 50 cm (19¾ in). Trim excess fabric, then overlock or zigzag raw edges. Turn the quilt to the right side.

19. Neatly slipstitch the opening closed and topstitch the quilt 5 mm (¼ in) from the seamline around all four sides.

VARIATIONS

❧ Use satin ribbon instead of the lace, or in addition to the lace, to decorate the squares.

❧ Use fabric in a different colour for the largest squares. I would suggest, however, that you do not create too strong a colour contrast, as this will tend to dominate.

❧ A double frill can be made by gathering 8 cm-wide (3¼ in-wide) lace with the calico frill, so that the lace lies on top of the calico.

❧ Stitch narrow crochet lace all along the edge of the calico frill.

WASHING YOUR COMFORTER

Try to choose a reasonably hot, windy day for washing your comforter. I have found that it is best to wash it by hand in a deep bath of cold, soapy water. Rinse the comforter thoroughly, removing any soapy residue, and squeeze out as much water as possible. Do not wring. If possible, spread the comforter over two parallel washing lines to dry. When dry, the comforter will show creases, but don't despair – these will gradually disappear without any ironing being required.

Work meticulously when ruching panels and lining up decorated squares.

FOUR-POSTER BEDS

Curtains around a bed were once considered a necessity, providing warmth and privacy. Today, they are rarely needed for such practical purposes, being chosen for their decorative value instead. With bedrooms being smaller and less elaborate, a grand four-poster is out of the question for most of us, but this does not mean that you cannot create a similar effect.

There are many different ways of dressing a four-poster bed. The most important factor to consider when choosing a design is the decor of the rest of the bedroom. Quite often all that is required is a length of fabric loosely draped around the frame. If you do decide to use more traditional valances and curtains, you may even find that you only need mock drops at the top end of the bed, rather than curtains at each of the four corners. If you want to create a highly romantic feel, use lots of lace.

FIGURE 1

MOCK CURTAINS AND VALANCES FOR A FOUR-POSTER BED

The instructions offer guidelines for decorating a double four-poster, with a top frame consisting of horizontal metal rods that can be temporarily removed and pushed through valance casings. The frame will have a valance all round, but curtains only at the top corners. These are mock curtains, or drapes that cannot be drawn around the bed.

REQUIREMENTS

(For dressing a double four-poster)

17 m x 150 cm-wide (18½ yd x 59 in-wide) calico
matching cotton thread
35 m x 6.5 cm-wide (38¼ yd x 2½ in-wide) edging lace

1. Begin by measuring the length and width of the top frame of the bed, i.e. the rods that will be covered by the valances (*see* Figure 1). I recommend using fabric double the length of the relevant rod for each valance, to allow for gathering.

2. Valances may differ in width, depending on the height of the frame. If your frame is very high, for instance, you have space for a relatively wide valance. I usually recommend a finished width of 35 cm (13¾ in) for a standard valance, and allow an additional 10 cm (4 in) for hems and casings. If your frame consists of large rods, you may need to allow extra fabric for wider casings. The casings for which instructions are given here accommodate rods with a diameter of 2 cm (¾ in).

3. Now that you have taken the necessary measurements, you can cut the calico that you will need for the valances. Cut two strips of calico, each measuring 45 cm (17¾ in) in width and double the length of the short sides of the frame. Cut a further two strips of calico, each measuring 45 cm (17¾ in) in width and double the length of the long sides of the frame, to allow for gathering.

4. The next step is to measure the length of the mock curtains. Measure the distance between the top of the rods and the floor (*see* Figure 1), and add 10 cm (4 in) to this measurement for hems and casings. This will give you the length of calico you need to cut for each curtain. For convenience, I usually use a width of 150 cm (59 in), which works well.

The Mock Curtains and Valances (page 58) of this four-poster bed contrast with the strong colour on the walls.

FIGURE 2

5. You will now need to make up four separate sections. The first section, section A (*see* Figures 2, 3a and 3b), consists of only a valance, to be used for the bottom end of the bed frame. The second and third sections, sections B and C (*see* Figures 2 and 4), which will be mirror images of each other, each consist of a valance with a curtain attached at the top end, to be used for the sides. The fourth section, section D (*see* Figures 2 and 5) consists of a valance with a curtain attached at each end, to be used for the top end of the frame.

6. To make section A, join strips of calico to obtain the required length (double the length of the rod). To determine how many strips of calico you need to cut, divide the total length required for this section by 150 cm (59 in). To determine the total amount of fabric required for this part of the frill, multiply the number of strips

by the full width of the frill, including the 10 cm (4 in) for casings and hems. Use French seams when joining (*see* Making a French Seam, page 8), overlock or zigzag each of the long sides, and turn over a double hem of 1 cm (⅜ in) to the wrong side at each short end (*see* Figure 3a).

7. Turn 8 cm (3¼ in) to the wrong side at the top of the valance, and, after turning under a 5 mm (¼ in) hem, stitch a casing of 4 cm (1½ in) (*see* Figure 3b). You should have a

heading of 3 cm (1¼ in) above the casing. Stitch 6.5 cm-wide (2½ in-wide) edging lace along the bottom edge of the valance.

8. To make sections B and C (*see* Figure 4), join strips of calico to obtain the required length for the valances on each side, as you did in Step 6. Use French seams when joining (*see* Making a French Seam, page 8), overlock or zigzag each of the long sides, and turn over a double hem of 1 cm (⅜ in) to the wrong side at each short end. Stitch a length of 6.5 cm-wide (2½ in-wide) edging lace along the bottom edge of each valance.

9. To make the curtains that form part of sections B and C, overlock or zigzag the top and bottom edges of two of the relevant lengths of calico. Turn over a double hem of 1 cm (⅜ in) to the wrong side down each of the long sides and stitch down. Determine which edge of each curtain will face inwards (i.e. towards the bottom of the bed), and stitch 6.5 cm-wide (2½ in-wide) edging lace all along it.

10. You now need to attach a valance to the outside of each of the two curtains, on the relevant side (either right or left, depending on the side of the bed on which the curtain will hang). Position the curtain right side up, and place the valance on top of it, also right side up, aligning the top edges (*see* Figure 4, page 61). Pin the two pieces of fabric together.

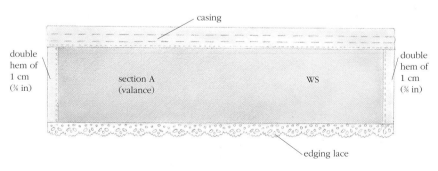

FIGURE 3A

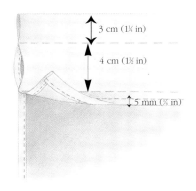

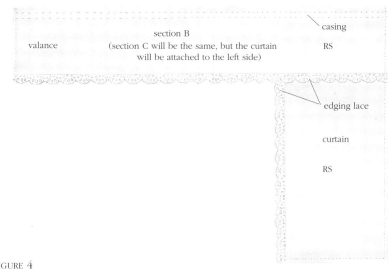

FIGURE 3B

11. For each of sections B and C, turn 8 cm (3¼ in) to the wrong side along the top edge, and, after turning under a 5 mm (¼ in) hem, stitch a casing of 4 cm (1½ in) (*see* Figure 3b, above). You should have a heading of approximately 3 cm (1¼ in) above the casing.

12. To make the valance for section D (*see* Figure 5), follow the instructions given in Step 6. Do not make the casing yet. Stitch 6.5 cm-wide (2½ in-wide) edging lace along the bottom edge of the valance as before (*see* Step 8).

13. To make the two curtains that form part of section D, overlock or zigzag the top and bottom edges of the two remaining lengths of calico. Turn over a double hem of 1 cm (⅜ in) to the wrong side down each of the long sides. Stitch down neatly. Determine which edge of each curtain will face inwards (i.e. away from the corners), and stitch 6.5 cm-wide (2½ in-wide) edging lace along these inner edges (*see* Figure 5).

14. Now you need to attach the valance to the outside of both curtains. Position the curtains right side up, and place the valance on top of them, also right side up, aligning the top edges and sides (*see* Figure 5). Pin each of the curtains to the valance in the correct position.

FIGURE 4

15. Turn over 8 cm (3¼ in) to the wrong side all along the top edge of both the curtains and the valance, and, after turning under and stitching a hem of 5 mm (¼ in), stitch a casing of 4 cm (1½ in) (*see* Figure 3b). As before, you should have a heading of 3 cm (1¼ in) above the casing.

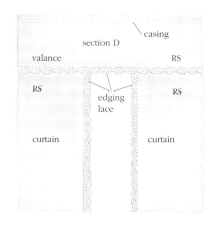

FIGURE 5

16. Remove one rod at a time from the frame of the bed, and push it through the casing of the relevant section (A, B, C or D). Replace each rod in turn and arrange the gathers of the valances and the curtains evenly along the rods. Measuring from the floor, carefully determine the length of your curtains and calculate the depth of the hem required. Remove the

curtains from the rods, turn up the required amount of fabric for the hems, and pin into position. Stitch down neatly and press.

17. Insert the rods into the casings again, as you did in Step 16, return the rods to their positions in the frame, and arrange the gathers of the fabric evenly once again.

18. Tie back the curtains, using padded bows (*see* Padded Bow, page 29) made of calico or fabric in the colour of your choice (*see* photograph, page 59).

VARIATIONS
❦ Calico is the ideal choice for this project, as it has no right or wrong side which one needs to take into account. If you decide to use a printed fabric, however, you will have to use two layers of fabric, wrong sides together, so that the wrong side of the fabric will not be visible on the inside.

❦ Use broderie anglaise along the edges of the valances and the curtains instead of edging lace.

❦ If you would like the bed to have a fuller, more luxurious look, and the proportions of the room allow it, use curtains at the bottom end of the bed as well, instead of just a valance.

MOCK SINGLE FOUR-POSTER BED

*Create this clever mock four-poster
using an ordinary single bed
for a lovely, feminine look
at minimal cost.*

Place an ordinary single bed in a corner of the room. Construct a very simple, but sturdy frame consisting of four wooden battens (*see* Figure 1 at the bottom of the page). Attach the frame to the walls and floor at the appropriate places using small metal brackets (*see* Figure 1).

Use your imagination to dress the frame, as you would dress a real four-poster bed (*see* photograph, page 59). When I made a mock four-poster for my daughter, I chose to use two valances, a curtain at each point of attachment to the wall, and two curtains at the outside corner (*see* illustration, right).

The valances can be gathered (remember to cut out fabric double the required finished length to allow for gathering) or, if your sewing machine has the facility, left flat and scalloped along the edges.

The width of the fabric required for the curtains will depend on how full you would like the finished curtains to be (again, remember to allow for gathering and seams). Make a neat double hem of 1 cm (⅜ in) along both long sides of each curtain.

Attach the curtains and then the valances to the painted frame using long strips of Velcro. The Velcro can be attached to the wooden battens using a simple staple gun or tiny nails. The curtains at the corner can be tied back using fabric bands to which bows can be attached. The two curtains against the walls can be held back using tiebacks (*see* Shaped Padded Tiebacks, page 81), which can be hooked to cup-hooks in the walls.

If the dimensions of the room allow it, create a romantic mock four-poster.

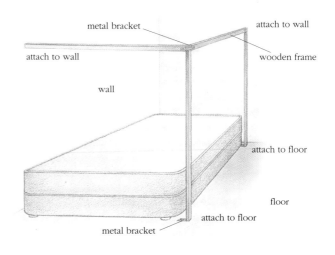

Figure 1

Transform your bedroom and create a striking corner using a Dolly Varden (page 64) dressed in calico.

COVERING A DOLLY VARDEN

*Currently there seems to be growing
interest in this once popular
dressing-table design. Rescue an old
dolly varden from the attic, or have
one constructed, and decorate it with
calico, lace and ribbon.*

*The basic woodwork required is very
simple. It needn't have drawers – a
few shelves on each side will do
(see Figure 1, page 65).*

*The kidney-shaped top is usually
made of pressed wood or chipboard.*

REQUIREMENTS

scrap paper large enough to make a template
of the top surface of the dolly varden
calico to cover the top of the dolly varden,
including a 1.5 cm (⅝ in) seam
allowance all round
matching cotton thread
piping for the circumference of the top
calico for the short frill
(double the circumference of the top in length
and roughly 15 cm (6 in) in width)
2.5 cm-wide (1 in-wide) edging lace to
decorate the edge of the short frill
1 cm-wide (⅜ in-wide) satin ribbon to
decorate the edge of the short frill

calico for the main frill
(double the circumference of the top in length,
and wide enough to reach the floor and
accommodate rufflette tape and a small hem
at the top or a casing to accommodate
the expanding wire and
a 3 cm-wide (1¼ in-wide) hem at the bottom
narrow rufflette tape or enough expanding wire
to fit around the circumference of the top
of the dolly varden when pulled taut
hooks and eyes, if using expanding wire
14 mm-wide (½ in-wide) satin ribbon
to decorate the bottom edge of the main frill
6.5 cm-wide (2½ in-wide) edging lace
to decorate the bottom edge of the main frill

This luxurious look has been achieved at minimal cost, combining calico, wide edging lace and satin ribbon.

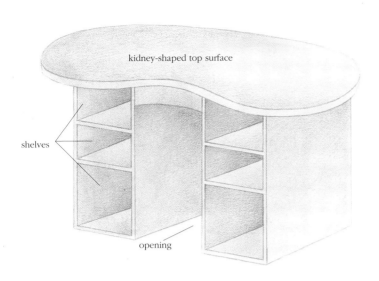

kidney-shaped top surface

shelves

opening

FIGURE 1

6. If your dolly varden has a curtain track, stitch narrow rufflette tape along the top edge of the frill and use curtain hooks. If there is no curtain track, make a 2 cm (¾ in) casing along the top edge of the frill by turning 1 cm (⅜ in) and then a further 2 cm (¾ in) to the wrong side and securing with a straight stitch. Feed the required length of expanding wire through the casing. Attach two small hooks at the centre front and two at each back corner to support the wire.

7. Make a hem of about 3 cm (1¼ in) along the bottom edge of the frill; then decorate with 2.5 cm-wide (1 in-wide) ribbon and 6.5 cm-wide (2½ in-wide) lace.

VARIATIONS

❧ Sew a pretty fabric bow (*see* Making a Fabric Bow, page 13) to the centre front of the short frill.

❧ Gather 8 cm-wide (3¼ in-wide) lace with the short frill to create a double frill, with the lace lying on top of the calico frill.

1. Start by making an accurate paper template of the kidney-shaped top surface of the dolly varden. Pin the template to the calico and cut out a piece of fabric to cover this area, allowing a 1.5 cm (⅜ in) seam allowance all round.

2. With the right sides and the raw edge of the piping and the calico together, pin the piping to the calico, the rounded edge of the piping facing inwards.

3. If necessary, join strips of calico to obtain the required length of fabric for the short frill. The frill should be about 15 cm (6 in) wide. Gather the frill to fit the circumference of the top (*see* Gathering a Frill, page 8) and pin into position, right side down, on top of the shaped top and the piping, aligning raw edges. Stitch down all round using the piping or zipper foot and join the two short ends using a French seam (*see* Making a French Seam, page 8). Overlock or zigzag the raw edges to neaten.

4. Decorate the edge of the short frill with 1 cm-wide (⅜ in-wide) ribbon and lace, positioning one edge of the ribbon over the raw edge of the lace, and stitching close to each edge of the ribbon.

5. Measure the required drop (width) of the main frill. If necessary, join sections of calico to obtain the required length of fabric for each half of the main frill. Do not stitch all the sections together to form a circle, as you will need an opening in the centre at the front to allow access to the shelves or drawers (*see* Figure 2).

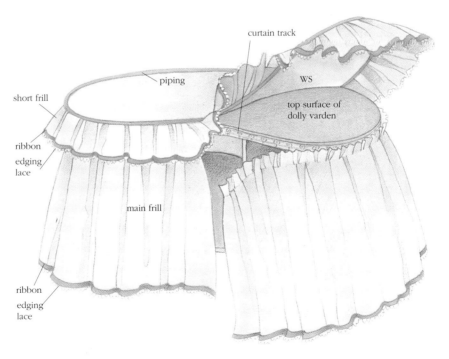

short frill

ribbon
edging
lace

main frill

ribbon
edging
lace

piping

curtain track

WS

top surface of
dolly varden

FIGURE 2

CHAPTER THREE

WINDOW-DRESSING

*T*he window-dressing is an important aspect of the decor of any room, so it deserves careful thought. Various options are available; your choice will depend on factors like the style of your house and the window, the size and colour scheme of the room, the style of the furniture, and, of, course, the cost involved. Calico, which lends itself to a variety of window treatments, and can be dressed up using piping, borders and frills in other fabrics, will satisfy even the most budget-conscious of home decorators.

CHOOSING YOUR WINDOW-DRESSING

No matter how beautiful your window-dressing is, it won't be successful if it doesn't fit in with the style of your home, or that of the window itself. Highlight beautiful woodwork or glass by downplaying the window-dressing, giving emphasis to the furniture and accessories instead. If you have attractive moulding around the window opening, consider using window-dressing that can be mounted within the window frame, so that the moulding will not be hidden.

The main function of a window is to provide natural light; the amount of light you receive will depend on the number of windows in the room, and their size, shape and location. To allow maximum light into the room, choose curtains that can be stacked or drawn back completely and a valance that hangs just a short distance into the window opening.

Look at the area surrounding the window. Ideally, there should be enough space to accommodate the stacked curtains, so that they do not block out the natural light when open. Where the space is limited, consider curtains that stack compactly. If you have a sliding door, you may consider extending the rail beyond the window on either side so that the curtains can be stacked or drawn away from the door when it is in use.

If you have windows of different styles or sizes in the same room, choose the same fabric for all the windows but consider using different styles of window-dressing – perhaps you could use full-length curtains for a large window, and a Roman blind or festoon blind for a small window.

If you decide to make curtains from calico, bear in mind that they will not block out light effectively. In a room such as a bedroom, where this is essential, I suggest

Bishop's Sleeve Curtains (page 76) create an opulent, luxurious setting.

that you consider using a blind made of a darker fabric in the window behind the calico curtains.

Another factor to consider when deciding on window-dressing is the importance of privacy in the room concerned. For maximum privacy, curtains and an inserted blind are an effective combination. Also remember that your choice of window-dressing should always look good from the outside as well as from the inside.

A few of the many window-dressing options available are discussed on this and the next page, and step-by-step instructions for making them are provided later in the chapter.

THE OPTIONS

Curtains are the most popular choice of window-dressing (*see* Lined Curtains, pages 72–73, and Unlined Curtains, page 73). Examples include café curtains, which cover the lower half of the window, ending at the sill, and short curtains, which end about 10 cm (4 in) below the window-sill. Full-length curtains, which can be tied back, lend themselves to both elegant and informal room settings, while extra-long curtains that puddle on the floor create a luxurious, theatrical mood.

Curtains can be combined with a valance, and with Roman or festoon blinds. They can also be decorated with a border in a contrasting fabric running down the centre and a bias binding edge along the top. Bedroom curtains look especially pretty with a frill down the centre edge.

A *valance* (*see* pages 84–86) which usually hangs from the front rail of a double track, hides the top of the curtains and gives more detail to the window-dressing. It can also be used to cover an ugly wooden or metal pelmet. In this case, expanding wire is threaded through a casing in the valance and pulled taut across the pelmet, or Velcro is used to attach the valance to the pelmet.

There is a range of styles to choose from: a shaped valance with a border; a straight valance with or without a border; a scalloped valance, and a valance with a frilled edge that can be straight or shaped.

The valance can be made in the same colour as the curtains, using a different colour for the border or frilled edge. Alternatively, use a contrasting fabric, repeating this fabric elsewhere in the room. Lined valances have more body and therefore hang better, and will also last longer.

Roman blinds (*see* pages 91–94) are perfect for windows that are no wider than 2.2 m (7 ft) and do not require too much dressing, and look most attractive fitted inside the window reveal. They are lined, and if measured and cut out accurately, work extremely well. Bear in mind, however, that the workings of the blind will be visible from the outside and need to be neat.

If you are going to use a Roman blind by itself, you may consider including a decorative feature like a contrasting border around all four sides, some pretty lace, or a scalloped edge. If, however, the blind is to be positioned within the window reveal, a straight edge is usually advisable.

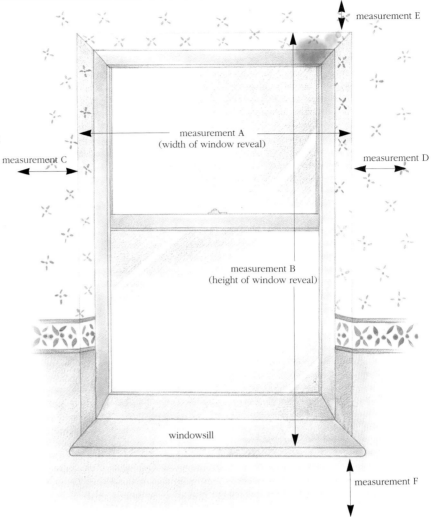

FIGURE 1

Festoon blinds (*see* pages 86–89) are frilly, puffy and cottagey, and can work well in any room. They are not suitable for windows wider than about 2.2 m (7 ft).

Mock festoon blinds (*see* pages 89–91) are perfect for a bathroom or toilet window, or wherever a working blind is not required. Once the tape has been gathered and the desired size and shape have been achieved, the blind is fixed in that position. Mock festoon blinds also make attractive valances.

Box-pleated festoon blinds (*see* pages 94–95) work on the same principle as festoon blinds, but create a more tailored look. They work well either fitted inside the window reveal, or hanging outside it.

London blinds, which have just two pleats – one on each side – are a combination of the Roman blind and the festoon blind in the sense that they are flat and not gathered, yet they create an attractive balloon effect at the bottom. They are best suited to rather narrow windows.

TAKING THE MEASUREMENTS

Once you have decided on your window treatment, carefully take the necessary measurements, using a metal tape measure if possible. Make a drawing of the window and record the dimensions in the relevant places (*see* Figure 1).

If your window-dressing is to be mounted inside the window reveal, measure only the width and the length of the opening (A and B).

If you have decided on window-dressing that will hang outside the window reveal, you need to measure the length and width of the opening (A and B), the area to be covered to the left and right of the window (C and D), and the area to be covered above and below the window (E and F).

CURTAINS

The following instructions on measuring windows and calculating fabric requirements will be very useful, whatever curtaining style you choose.

MEASUREMENTS AND CALCULATIONS

Referring to Figure 1 on page 69, carefully write down the required measurements. As a rough guide, I usually allow 20 cm (8 in) above the window (E). For full-length curtains, measure from the sill to halfway down the skirting board. The space available on either side of the window will obviously determine measurements C and D, but 15–25 cm (6–10 in) is the norm. Once you have taken all the measurements, add them up to determine the finished width and length of the curtain.

To calculate the number of drops (widths of fabric) you will need, refer to your diagram and add measurements C, D and A together; this will be the finished width of your curtains. Multiply this measurement by 2 to allow for gathering; if you are going to use prong tape instead of two- or three-cord heading tape, multiply this measurement by 2.5. Divide the answer by the width of the

fabric (calico is normally 150 cm [59 in] wide). The result will give you an indication of the number of drops you need. If the answer is 2.6, for example, it will be best to use three drops, which will give you a fuller effect. This means that you will need one and a half drops for each curtain. Joining drops is discussed in the box on the right.

To calculate the cutting length of each drop, refer to your diagram and add measurements E, B and F together. Add 18 cm (7 in) to each drop to allow for the hem at the bottom and the heading at the top.

For example: if your finished width equals 2.25 m (88½ in), and the finished length equals 2.2 m (86½ in/2½ yd), you will need to cut three drops ([2.25 m x 2] divided by 150 cm = 3, or [88½ in x 2] divided by 59 in = 3) of 2.38 m (93½ in) each (2.2 m plus 18 cm, or 86½ in plus 7 in).

HEADING TAPE

❦ Standard two-cord heading tape is usually used for curtains that will hang behind a pelmet. I also use it to make the vertical rows on mock festoon blinds as it gathers up nicely and creates the right effect.

❦ Three-cord heading tape is best for full-length curtains that will hang on a rail.

To attach two- or three-cord heading tape to the curtain, fold the required amount of fabric to the wrong side along the top of the curtain and press; position the tape about 2 cm (¾ in) below the fold, turning under a short section of tape at the beginning and at the end, and making sure that the raw edge of the curtain is covered by the tape. Stitch close to both sides of the tape. At the centre edge of the curtain, tuck under the end of the tape, and stitch down, thus securing the cords. On the outside edge, pull a short section of each

JOINING DROPS

If, as in the example on the left, you determine that you require a total of three drops to cover your window, it will be necessary to join full drops and half-drops.

Cut three drops to the required cutting length, then cut one of the drops in half lengthwise. With the right sides together, attach one half-drop to each full drop, making sure that the joins will be positioned nearer to the outside edge than the centre of each curtain when completed. Overlock or zigzag to neaten the seams and press open or to one side.

The same procedure should be followed for joining two drops of different widths – the narrower of the two should be halved, and one half should be attached to each side of the wider, central drop. The procedure for joining drops of equal width is exactly the same, except that of course the join will be positioned in the centre of the curtain.

To avoid having to finish raw edges after joining drops, make use of selvedges wherever you possibly can.

cord out, hold the cords away from the edge to avoid catching them in the stitching line, then tuck the end under and stitch.

Once the heading is complete, measure the length of the curtain, from the middle of the heading tape to the bottom of the curtain, and subtract the desired finished length from this measurement. This will give you the depth of your hem at the bottom of the curtain. (Though you will have allowed for the hem before cutting out, it is wise to measure again at this stage.) It is always a good idea to pin the hem into position and then to hang the curtain, making adjustments if necessary. This avoids having to unpick later!

Skilful window-dressing can make a narrow window seem wider.

To make a pocket for the cords that hang loose once the curtain tape has been gathered, cut a rectangle of calico measuring 15 cm x 10 cm (6 in x 4 in). Hem one short side, then fold the rectangle in half, right sides together, bringing the hemmed side up to lie 5 mm (⅛ in) short of the other short side. Leaving this side open, stitch up the two remaining sides to form a pocket. Turn to the right side and press.

Before stitching down the curtain tape, slip the raw edge of the pocket under the bottom edge of the tape, then straight stitch along this edge to attach both the tape and the pocket. Attach the pocket to the outside edge of the curtain, where the cords will hang.

made of frosted glass. On the other hand, lining increases the lifespan of the fabric, adds body – which helps to make the curtain hang better – provides insulation and added privacy, and generally gives a more professional finish.

Fabric used for lining should be of good quality and should be preshrunk. Preferably, use the same type of fabric as you used for the curtains themselves, i.e. if using cotton for the curtains, use a cotton or polycotton lining too. Save time by using lining that is the same width as the main fabric.

Lining can be attached to the curtain or left loose. I generally leave it loose, as I find that curtains with attached lining tend to bubble. Instead, I use French tacks to make shanks that hold the lining in position at regular intervals (*see* page 73). Also, if the lining is not of good quality fabric, problems might arise when the curtains are washed, for instance if the lining shrinks much more than the curtaining fabric.

❦ Deep pleat or prong tape is used for hanging curtains from a wooden or brass rod and helps to create a fairly tailored look. Instead of multiplying your width by 2 to obtain the width of fabric required, multiply by 2.5, as you will need more fabric for the pleats than you would use for making curtains with two- or three-cord heading tape.

LINING

It is, of course, much quicker and easier not to line curtains; but give the matter some careful thought before you make your decision. Unlined curtains are great in an area that does not get much sunlight, where privacy is not an issue, or where the window is

LINED CURTAINS

To facilitate accurate planning, draw a diagram of your window and record the relevant measurements in the appropriate places (see Figure 1, page 69).

REQUIREMENTS

calico (*see* Figure 1, page 69 and Step 1, below)
matching cotton thread
polycotton for lining
three-cord heading tape

1. Cut the number of drops required to make up a total width of double the length of the curtain rail, and add 18 cm (7 in) to the length for the headings and the hems.

2. With right sides together, join the required number of drops for each curtain (*see* Joining Drops, page 70).

3. Turn 1 cm (⅜ in) to the wrong side along both long sides of each curtain and press. Now turn over a further 2.5 cm (1 in) and press again. Blind stitch or straight stitch the hems into position.

4. Using the polycotton, cut the required number of drops; the lining should be the same width as the curtain, but 10 cm (4 in) shorter. Join the drops for the lining (*see* Joining Drops, page 70). Stitch a 5 cm (2 in) hem down both long sides of the lining. Turn a hem of 1 cm (⅜ in) and then a further 6 cm (2¼ in) to the wrong side along the bottom edge of the lining and stitch.

5. With wrong sides together, lay the lining on the curtain and pin into position. If you intend making a little pocket for storing the cords once the heading has been gathered, do so at this stage (*see* Making a Pocket for the Curtain Cords, page 71). Along the top edge of both the curtain and the lining, turn over 5 cm (2 in) and press. Position and then pin the three-cord heading tape 2 cm (¾ in) below the

Lined Curtains hang well, look professional and offer insulation.

fold, tucking under a short section of tape at the beginning and the end. Make sure that the raw edges of the fabric are covered by the tape (*see* Figure 1, right). Stitch the tape (*see* Heading Tape, page 70) and the pocket for the curtain cords (if you have made one) into position at the same time.

6. Measure from the middle of the heading tape to the bottom of the curtain and subtract the desired finished length of the curtain from this measurement to determine the final depth of the hem. (Although

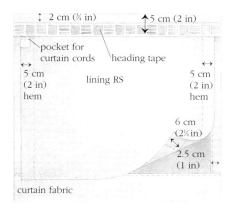

FIGURE 1

you allowed for a hem when cutting out, it is best to re-measure at this stage.) Fold under 2 cm (¾ in) along the raw edge and press. Fold, press and pin the hem into position, then straight stitch or blind stitch.

7. Lay the curtain flat, wrong side up, and make shanks at 30–50 cm (12–20 in) intervals down the sides of the curtain (*see* Using French Tacks to Make Shanks, below). These attach the curtain to the lining, giving your curtaining a professional finish.

USING FRENCH TACKS TO MAKE SHANKS

French tacks, which are used to attach the lining to the curtain, should be positioned along the outer hem of the curtain so that they can be sewn through two thicknesses of fabric, without being visible from the right side.

To make a shank, make a small stitch through the curtain hem, and another through the lining, opposite the first stitch. Leave a short section of thread, 2–4 cm (¾–1½ in) in length, between the two stitches. Repeat the procedure several times, until you have a few long 'stitches' between the curtain fabric and the lining. Bind them using a row of blanket stitches, worked close together.

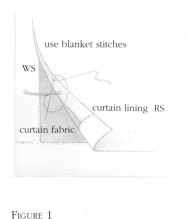

use blanket stitches

WS

curtain lining RS

curtain fabric

FIGURE 1

UNLINED CURTAINS

Referring to Figure 1 on page 69, draw a diagram of your window and record the required measurements taken in the appropriate places.

REQUIREMENTS

calico (*see* Figure 1, page 69, and Step 1, below)
matching cotton thread
two-cord heading tape

1. Calculate how many drops you need to cover the width of the window by dividing the cutting width (i.e the width of fabric you need before gathering) by the width of the fabric. As one generally uses narrower heading tape for unlined curtains you need add only 12 cm (4¾ in) to the finished length to obtain the cutting length of the drops.

2. With right sides together, join the drops to obtain the required width for each curtain (*see* Joining Drops, page 70).

3. Turn under a hem of 1 cm (⅜ in) down both long sides of each curtain and press. Turn under a further 2.5 cm (1 in); press again and blind stitch or straight stitch the hems into position.

4. Position the curtain wrong side up. If you intend making a little pocket in which to store the cords once the heading has been gathered, do so at this stage (*see* Making a Pocket for the Curtain Cords, page 71). Along the top edge, turn over 3 cm (1¼ in) and press. Position and then pin the two-cord heading tape 2 cm (¾ in) below the fold, tucking under a short section of tape at the beginning and at the end. The raw edge of the curtain should be covered by the tape. Stitch the tape into position (*see* Heading Tape, page 70).

5. Measure the length of the curtain from the middle of the heading tape to the bottom, and subtract the desired finished length of the curtain from this measurement to determine the final depth of the hem. (Although you allowed for a hem when cutting out, it is best to re-measure at this stage.) Fold under 2 cm (¾ in) along the raw edge and press, then fold, press and pin the hem into position. Straight stitch or blind stitch to complete the hem.

ROD POCKET CURTAINS

As the name suggests, a wooden rod housed in a pocket or casing is used for this very simple style of curtaining; bear in mind, however, that these curtains are not suitable for windows wider than about 150 cm (5 ft). A heading above the casing forms an attractive ruffle when the rod is inserted into the casing. Remember that the casing must be large enough to accommodate the rod comfortably and allow the curtain to gather on the rod.

REQUIREMENTS

calico (see Lined Curtains, page 72, or Unlined Curtains, this page, and Step 1, below)
matching cotton thread
polycotton for lining (optional)

1. When calculating how many drops you require, multiply the length of the rod (*see* Figure 1, page 74) by 2 or 2.5, depending on the fullness required, and divide this total by the width of your fabric. To calculate the cutting length of your curtains, add 14 cm (5½ in) for the heading, casing and top hem, and a further 12 cm (4¾ in) for the bottom hem to the desired finished length. (Adjust the casing measurement to fit the size of your curtain rod.)

2. With right sides together, join the drops to obtain the required width for each curtain (*see* Joining Drops, page 70).

3. Turn under a hem of 1 cm (⅜ in) down both long sides of each curtain and press. Turn under a further 2.5 cm (1 in); press again and blind stitch or straight stitch the hems into position.

4. If you would like to line your curtains, cut out the required number of drops from the polycotton; the lining should be the same width as the curtain, and 10 cm (4 in) shorter. Join the drops (*see* Joining Drops, page 70) and complete the side hems, turning 5 cm (2 in) to the wrong side. With wrong sides together, and aligning raw edges at the top, place the lining on top of the curtain, and pin into position.

5. Overlock or zigzag the top edge of each curtain, then fold over 1 cm (⅜ in) to form a hem, press and straight stitch into position. Now turn over a further 13 cm (5 in) and press. Straight stitch 1 cm from the lower edge to form a casing. In a line parallel to this, straight stitch 3 cm (1¼ in) below the folded edge at the top, forming a heading of 3 cm (1¼ in) and a casing of 9 cm (3¾ in) in the process (*see* Figure 2).

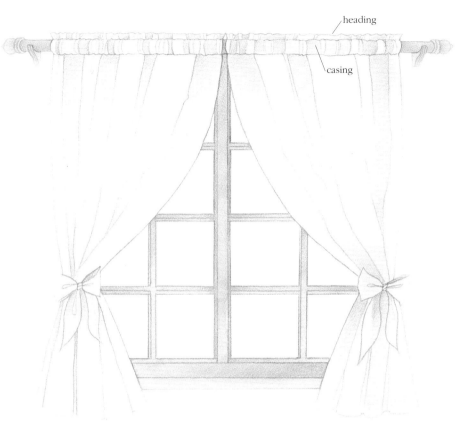

FIGURE 1

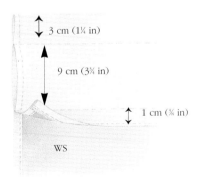

FIGURE 2

6. Complete by making a hem along the bottom edge of each curtain (measuring from the bottom of the casing), following the instructions for Lined Curtains on page 72, or Unlined Curtains on page 73. If you have made curtains with a lining, complete the bottom hem of the lining following the instructions given for Lined Curtains on page 72.

ROD SLEEVE CURTAINS

If you are making rod pocket curtains that don't meet in the centre, but just hang decoratively at the sides, make a sleeve for the central part of the rod, which will be exposed (see Figure 1 on page 76). Remember that the heading allowed for the curtains should be the same for the centre sleeve so that the impression is given that the sleeve is a continuation of the curtains. Equal headings above and below the sleeve work well.

REQUIREMENTS

calico (see Lined Curtains, page 72, or Unlined Curtains, page 73, and Steps 1 and 4, below)
matching cotton thread
polycotton for lining (optional)

1. As these are not working curtains (*see* Figure 1 on page 76), the same fullness is not required and one drop per curtain will be sufficient. To the desired finished length of your curtain, add 14 cm (5½ in); i.e. 1 cm (⅜ in) for the top hem, 3 cm (1¼ in) for the heading, and 10 cm (4 in) for the casing for the curtain rod. (Adjust the casing measurement for a thinner or thicker rod.) Add a further 12 cm (4¾ in) to the length measurement for the bottom hem, and cut out your fabric.

2. Turn under a hem of 1 cm (⅜ in) down the long sides of each curtain and press. Turn under a further 2.5 cm (1 in), then press and blind stitch or straight stitch into position.

3. If you would like to line your curtains, cut out the required number of drops from the polycotton; the lining should be the same width as the curtain, and 10 cm (4 in) shorter. Join the drops (*see* Joining Drops, page 70) and complete the side hems, turning 5 cm (2 in) to the wrong side. With wrong sides together, and raw edges aligned at the top, place the lining on top of the curtain, and pin into position.

4. Zigzag or overlock the top edge of each curtain, fold over 1 cm (⅜ in), press and straight stitch the hem into position. Now fold over a further 13 cm (5 in). Straight stitch 1 cm from the lower edge of this casing. In a line parallel to this, straight stitch 3 cm (1¼ in) below the folded edge at the top, forming a heading of 3 cm (1¼ in) and a casing of 9 cm (3¾ in) in the process (*see* Figure 2, page 74).

5. Complete by making a hem along the bottom edge of each curtain (measuring from the bottom of the casing), following the instructions for Lined Curtains on page 72, or Unlined Curtains on page 73. If you have made curtains with a lining, complete the bottom hem of the lining following the instructions given for Lined Curtains on page 72.

6. For the central section, you will need a tube to accommodate the exposed part of the curtain rod (*see* Figure 1, page 76). Cut a rectangle of calico measuring double the length of the exposed rod plus 2 cm (¾ in) in length, and 36 cm (14 in) in width, i.e. (10 cm [4 in] for the casing plus 6 cm [2¼ in] for the top and bottom headings and 2 cm [¾ in] for the seam joining the two long sides of the tube) x 2. Adjust the casing measurement for a thinner or thicker rod if necessary. Fold 1 cm (⅜ in) to the wrong side along each short side of the rectangle; press and stitch,

Rod Pocket Curtains (page 73) form an attractive ruffle above the rod.

rod sleeve

casing

FIGURE 1

using a straight stitch. With right sides together, and using a 1 cm (⅜ in) seam, join the two long sides of the rectangle together to form a tube. Now carefully turn the tube to the right side.

7. Making sure that the join in the tube will be positioned at the back of the rod, straight stitch 3 cm (1¼ in) from both the top and the bottom edge of the tube (through both thicknesses), thereby forming two headings with a 10 cm (4 in) casing between them.

8. Feed the curtain rod through one curtain casing, then the sleeve, and lastly through the second curtain casing. Arrange the gathers evenly along the rod.

9. Tie the curtains back with attractive swag holders or tiebacks, attaching fabric bows (*see* Making a Fabric Bow, page 13) if you like.

BISHOP'S SLEEVE CURTAINS

Requiring generous amounts of fabric, this style is suitable for an opulent, luxurious, room setting (see photograph, page 68).

Make the curtains in the usual way (*see* Lined Curtains, page 72, or Unlined Curtains, page 73), adding about 15 cm (6 in) to the cutting length of the curtain and lining, if using, to allow for blousing once the curtain has been tied back. If you want the curtains to puddle on the floor, add a further 20 cm (8 in) to the cutting length.

Once complete, hang the curtain on the rod or rail, lift it so that it blouses nicely, and tie back with an attractive cord or swag holder (available from most suppliers of curtaining materials). Arrange the puddle of fabric (if using) on the floor, and stand back to admire!

CURTAINS WITH FRILLED EDGES

Curtains with frilled edges create a really cottagey look and are particularly suitable for bedroom, kitchen or bathroom windows. For practical purposes, the windows should not generally be wider than about 180 cm (6 ft) and the drop of the curtains should not be less than about 120 cm (4 ft). As these curtains look best in a tied-back position, they work well in a situation where they can be left open permanently.
If privacy is required, the curtains can be combined with a blind.
In addition, they can be co-ordinated with tie-backs that also have a frilled edge.
If the curtains are going to hang all the way to the floor, it is best to have frills down the centre only.
If they hang just past the sill, stitch a frill down the centre and along the bottom edge of the curtains, rounding the inside bottom corners slightly. Another idea is to overlap the tops of the curtains by about 20 cm (8 in), and then to stitch the two curtains together using one continuous row of tape (see Figure 1, page 78).

REQUIREMENTS

calico (*see* Lined Curtains, page 72, or Unlined Curtains, page 73, and Steps 1 and 2, below)
matching cotton thread
polycotton for lining (optional)
two- or three-cord heading tape

1. After completing the necessary measurements and calculations, cut out the required number of drops for the curtains.

2. To calculate how much fabric you need for the frill down the centre and along the bottom of one curtain, add the cutting length to the cutting width of the curtain, and multiply the result by 2 to allow for gathering. (If you are attaching a frill to the centre edge

Curtains with Frilled Edges combined with a deep, full valance are a good choice for a bathroom.

only, use just the cutting length of the curtain, and multiply by 2.) This will give you the length of the frill before gathering. To decide how many strips of fabric you will need to make up this length, divide the total length of the frill by the width of the fabric. Decide on the depth of the frill you would like (10 cm [4 in] works well) and add 1 cm (⅜ in) to this measurement for the seam allowance and 1 cm (⅜ in) for the hem. This is for a single-thickness frill; if you want a fold-over frill, cut it double the required finished width, adding 2 cm (¾ in) for seam allowances.

3. Join all the strips for the frill together using French seams (*see* Making a French Seam, page 8). For a fold-over frill, fold the long strip so that its width is halved, with the wrong sides together and the joins on the inside. Press, then straight stitch the long raw edges together. For a single-thickness frill, overlock or zigzag along one raw edge of the strip and then fold over a 1 cm (⅜ in) hem.

4. Whether you are making a single-thickness frill or a fold-over frill, gather the strip to half the cutting length along the raw edge. (*see* Gathering a Frill, page 8.)

5. If you are using more than one drop per curtain, join the required number of drops together (*see* Joining Drops, page 70). If you are attaching the frill down the centre and along the bottom edge, place one curtain on top of the other, right sides together and, using a soft pencil and an object with a curved edge (a dinner or side plate works well), draw a gentle curve on the inside bottom corner of the top curtain. Trim away the excess through both layers.

6. With the wrong side uppermost, turn under and press 1 cm (⅜ in) and then a further 2.5 cm (1 in)

along the outside edge of each curtain. Blind stitch or straight stitch into position.

7. Starting at the top of each of the curtains, with the right sides of the curtain and the frill together, pin and stitch the frill, along its gathered edge, down the centre edge of the curtain, around the shaped bottom corner and across the bottom. Overlock or zigzag the raw edges of the curtain and frill. (If attaching the frill down the centre edge only, stop when you reach the bottom of the curtain.)

8. If you are using a lining, attach it at this stage. Join the required number of drops to achieve the same cutting width as each curtain, and hem the long outside edge. With right sides together, position the lining on top of the curtain, and pin along the edges. Working on the wrong side of the curtain, with the frill neatly tucked in and lying towards the curtain, stitch the lining to the curtain all along the stitching line created when the frill was attached. If necessary, trim the lining to the size and shape of the curtain and overlock or zigzag all three edges together.

9. Working on the wrong side, open out the frill, away from the curtain (and the lining, if using) and press the seam allowance towards the curtain. On the right side of the curtain, topstitch about 5 mm (¼ in) from the seam. You may wish to stitch lace to the edge of a single-thickness frill.

10. Lay the curtain down flat, wrong side up. Using a metal tape measure, and working from the bottom of the curtain to the top, mark the finished length of the curtain. Measure and mark the top hem, making sure that it will be wide enough to accommodate the heading tape, which will be positioned 2 cm (¾ in) below the fold. Before folding, cut off any excess fabric if necessary. If you intend making a little pocket in which to store the cords once the tape has been gathered, do so at this stage (*see* Making a Pocket for the Curtain Cords, page 71).

11. Fold over the allowance for the top hem and position the heading tape 2 cm (¾ in) below the fold right across the curtain and the frill, tucking under a short section of tape at the beginning and the

end. Make sure that the raw edges of the curtain are covered by the tape. Stitch the tape into position (*see* Heading Tape, page 70).

12. For full-length curtains without a frill along the bottom, complete the hem, following the instructions for Lined Curtains on page 72, or for Unlined Curtains on page 73.

VARIATION
❧ If you would like your curtains to overlap (*see* Figure 1, below), complete Step 10, then determine the depth of the overlap. I usually find that overlapping the curtains by about a third of their width (*see* Figure 1) works well. Lay the curtains flat, wrong sides up, overlapping them by the desired distance. Pin the two curtains together in this position. Fold over the allowance for the top hem and position the heading tape 2 cm (¾ in) below the fold right across both curtains and the frill (*see* Figure 1), tucking under a short section of the tape at the beginning and the end. Ensure that the tape covers the raw edges, and stitch down neatly.

CURTAINS WITH A CONTRASTING BORDER

A contrasting border can add a lovely finishing touch to your curtains. This border is stitched down the centre edge of the curtain; at the bottom, it wraps around to the wrong side of the curtain.

REQUIREMENTS

calico (*see* Lined Curtains, page 72, or Unlined Curtains, page 73)
matching cotton thread
contrasting fabric for border
polycotton for lining (optional)
two- or three-cord heading tape

1. After completing the necessary measurements and calculations, cut out the required number of

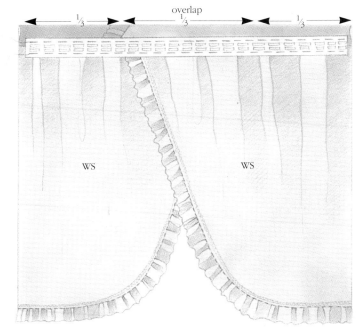

FIGURE 1

drops. Join the drops to make up the required width for each curtain (*see* Joining Drops, page 70). Turn 1 cm (⅜ in) to the wrong side along the long outside edge of each curtain and press. Turn over a further 2.5 cm (1 in) and press again. Stitch to hem.

2. For each curtain, prepare a strip of fabric in a contrasting colour for the border. The cutting width of the strip should be twice the desired finished width, plus 2 cm (¾ in). The cutting length of the strip will be equal to the cutting length of the curtain. If possible, cut one continuous strip down the length of the fabric to avoid a join.

3. With wrong sides together, fold the strip so that its width is halved, and press. With the right sides of the strip and the curtain together, and the raw edges aligned at the top and sides, pin and stitch the contrast border to the centre edge of the curtain (*see* Figure 1). Stitch right to the end of the border, leaving a seam allowance of 1 cm (⅜ in). Trim the seam allowance to 5 mm (¼ in) and neaten raw edges.

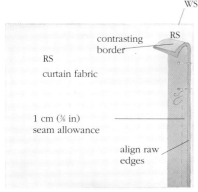

FIGURE 1

4. If you are going to line your curtains, complete Steps 5 and 6 before completing Step 4. With the curtain wrong side up, open the contrast border away from the curtain and press the seam allowance towards the curtain.

Use Curtains with a Contrasting Border to introduce colour and add interest.

Working on the right side of the curtain, topstitch about 5 mm (¼ in) from the seamline.

5. Turn under 2 cm (¾ in) and then a further 10 cm (4 in) along the bottom edge of the curtains; press and then blind stitch or straight stitch into position.

6. If you are going to line your curtains, join drops to obtain the desired width, if necessary (*see* Joining Drops, page 70), and turn over a 5 cm (2 in) hem on each long side. Complete the bottom hem of the lining so that it is 4 cm (1½ in) shorter than the curtain. With right sides together, place the lining on top of the curtain, and pin into position. Working on the wrong side of the front of the curtain, with the border lying towards the curtain, stitch the lining to the curtain along the line of stitching attaching the border to the curtain. Neaten raw edges down the centre. Topstitch as described before (Step 4).

7. Lay the curtain down flat, wrong side up. Using a metal tape measure, and working from the bottom of the curtain to the top, mark the finished length of the curtain. Measure and mark the position of the heading, making sure that it will be wide enough to accommodate the heading tape, which will be positioned 2 cm (¾ in) below the fold. Cut off any excess fabric if necessary. If you intend making a little pocket in which to store the cords once the tape has been gathered, do so at this stage (*see* Making a Pocket for the Curtain Cords, page 71). Fold over the allowance for the top hem and pin the curtain tape into position, tucking a short section of the tape under at the beginning and the end. Make sure that the raw edge of the curtain (and the lining, if you are using one) is covered by the tape. Stitch the tape into position (*see* Heading Tape, page 70).

Curtains with a Contrasting Band are suited to a more modern setting.

CURTAINS WITH A CONTRASTING BAND

A band in a contrasting fabric is attached to the front of the curtain, usually about 10 cm (4 in) from the centre edge.

REQUIREMENTS

calico (*see* Lined Curtains, page 72, or Unlined Curtains, page 73)
matching cotton thread
contrasting fabric for band
polycotton for lining (optional)
two- or three-cord heading tape

1. After completing the necessary measurements and calculations (*see* Lined Curtains, page 72, or Unlined Curtains, page 73), join the number of drops required to obtain the desired width for each curtain (*see* Joining Drops, page 70). Turn 1 cm (⅜ in) to the wrong side along both long sides of each curtain and press. Turn over a further 2.5 cm (1 in) and press again. Blind stitch or straight stitch the hems into position.

2. For each curtain, cut a strip of fabric in a contrasting colour, adding 4 cm (1½ in) to the desired finished width of the band to obtain the cutting width. Cut the strip to the same cutting length as the curtain. It is preferable to cut one continuous strip down the length of the fabric so that joins will not be necessary.

3. Press 2 cm (¾ in) to the wrong side along both long edges of your contrasting band.

4. With the curtain right side up, decide on the position of the contrasting band – I find that it looks best 10 cm (4 in) from the centre edge of the curtain. Make a soft pencil line in this position down the length of the curtain.

5. With raw edges aligned at the top, pin the contrasting band, wrong side down, to the right side of the curtain, positioning the folded right-hand edge of the band along the pencil line. Working on the right side, topstitch the band down along both sides, about 5 mm (¼ in) from the edge (*see* Figure 1, below).

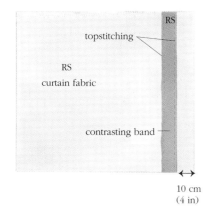

FIGURE 1

6. Attach the lining, if you are using one, and the heading tape and complete the bottom hem following the instructions for Lined Curtains on page 72, or for Unlined Curtains on page 73.

TIEBACKS

Tiebacks can round off the window-dressing nicely. They add decorative detail and a professional finish, but are also practical in that they hold the curtains back to allow the light in during the day.
The position of the tieback determines the silhouette of the curtain. It is usually placed about two-thirds down the length of the curtain. Tiebacks can be made in the same fabric as the curtain, or in a contrasting fabric – if, for instance, the window has a valance, the fabric used for the valance can be repeated in the tieback.

SHAPED PADDED TIEBACKS

Use these curved, padded tiebacks for short or floor-length curtains. To determine the length of the tieback, draw and stack the curtain, then loosely loop a tape measure around the curtain, holding the ends where the finished tieback will be hooked to the wall. This will be the length of your tieback.

REQUIREMENTS

scrap paper for template
enough fabric for two tiebacks (four pieces make two tiebacks)
compressed wadding for two tiebacks (two pieces)
matching cotton thread
bias binding to fit the circumference of each tieback
four small plastic rings
one tieback hook for each tieback

1. Trace off the template supplied on page 82, adjusting the shape if you like, and lengthening or shortening it to suit your particular requirements.

2. Fold the main fabric in half, right sides together, and position the straight edge of the template

on the fold of the fabric. Cut out four identical curved shapes using the template. Open out.

3. Cut out two pieces of wadding to the same size and shape as the pieces of fabric.

4. For each tieback, pin all three layers together (two main fabric sections, with wadding between them) so that on both sides the right side of the main fabric is on the outside.

5. Stitch the three layers together 1 cm (⅜ in) from the edge, pivoting your work as you stitch around the corners. Trim the seam allowance to 5 mm (¼ in).

6. Stitch the bias binding all the way round the tieback to cover the raw edges. Position the join in the bias binding where it will not be noticed, and join neatly.

7. Hand stitch a small plastic ring to each end of the tieback, so that the rings will not be visible when the tieback is seen from the front (*see* Figure 1, below, for positioning).

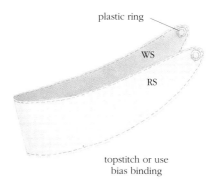

FIGURE 1

These rings will be hooked to the tieback hook on the wall when the curtains are open. Ensure that you stitch the rings to the relevant sides of the tiebacks, depending on whether the tieback is to be hooked to the left or to the right.

8. Screw the tieback hook into the wall in the appropriate position.

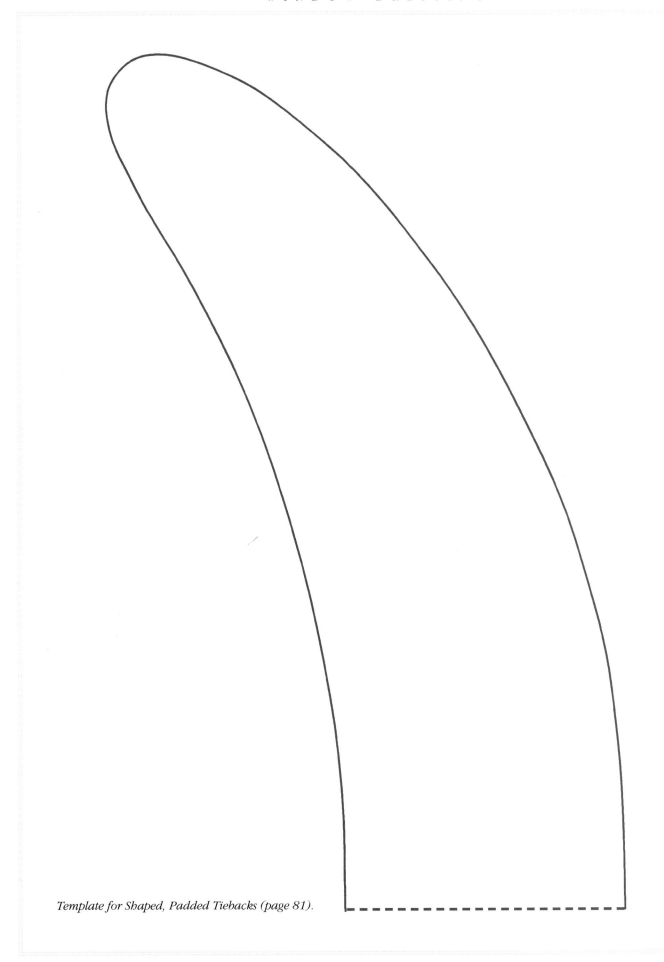

Template for Shaped, Padded Tiebacks (page 81).

9. Repeat the whole process to complete the second tieback, ensuring that you sew the plastic rings to the appropriate sides.

VARIATIONS

❧ Simple topstitching all around the edges of the tieback can also work well, instead of bias binding.

❧ Make a fabric bow (*see* Making a Fabric Bow, page 13) using the same fabric as the tieback, or a contrasting colour, and hand stitch this to the front of the tieback, close to where the tieback will be hooked to the wall.

❧ Make a lovely, feminine tieback using lace and ribbon to decorate the right side of the tieback.

❧ Stitch piping around the tieback instead of bias binding. To do so, place one layer of main fabric, wrong side down, on a piece of wadding; pin and stitch all the way round. Working on the right side of the fabric, with the raw edges of the piping and the fabric together, pin and stitch the piping around the edge of the fabric (*see* Figure 2), using the piping or zipper foot of your machine. With right sides together, pin the second piece of main fabric to the first. Working on the wadding, stitch all three layers together along the existing stitching line, using your piping or zipper foot; leave an opening of about 10 cm (4 in). Turn to the right side, press, and neatly slipstitch the opening closed.

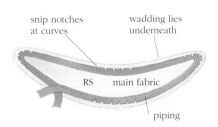

snip notches at curves
wadding lies underneath
RS   main fabric
piping

FIGURE 2

PLAITED TIEBACKS

Plaited tiebacks can be made up of calico or of fabric in three different colours or patterns. Determine the finished length following the instructions for Shaped Padded Tiebacks on page 81.

REQUIREMENTS

24 cm x 150 cm-wide (9½ in x 59 in-wide) calico, or fabric in three different colours or patterns (this will be sufficient for two tiebacks)
matching cotton thread
polyester filling or scraps of wadding
scraps of 2 mm-thick (⅛ in-thick) nylon cord
four small plastic rings
one tieback hook for each tieback

1. Add 15 cm (6 in) to the circumference of the stacked curtain, and cut one piece of fabric to this length and to a width of 24 cm (9½ in). Repeat for the other two colours. Cut each piece in half down the centre. You should now have six lengths of fabric, each 12 cm (4¾ in) wide; you will use three for each tieback.

2. With right sides together, fold each strip of fabric, halving its width. With a 1 cm (⅜ in) seam allowance, stitch down the length of the strip and across one end, leaving an opening at the other end. Turn the tube to the right side and press.

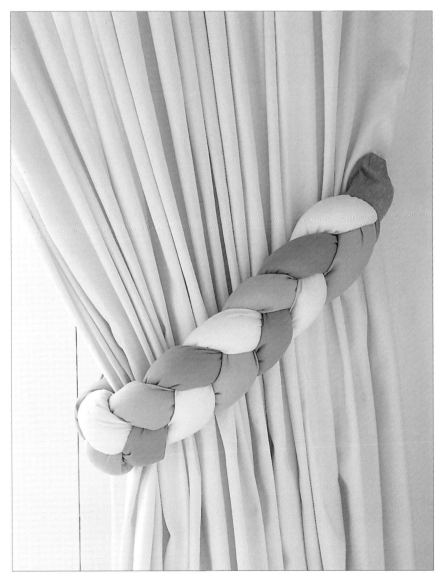

Three different colours have been used in this Plaited Tieback.

3. Fill each tube with polyester filling or scraps of wadding. The tubes should be firm, but not too stiff and full, or it will be difficult to plait the tiebacks. Neatly hand stitch the open ends closed.

4. Cut four squares of calico, each measuring 12 cm x 12 cm (4¾ in x 4¾ in). Fold each square over, right sides together, and stitch the short sides together. Turn right side out.

5. Position the first set of three tubes so that the top ends overlap one another, as you would in preparation for plaiting. Secure by tying with a short length of nylon cord, elastic or cotton thread. Place one of the squares over the secured ends of the tubes. Slip stitch into position, tucking under a 1 cm (⅜ in) hem as you stitch.

A Shaped Valance with a Border (page 85) adds a special finishing touch.

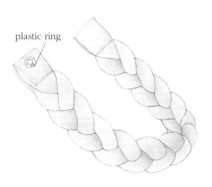

plastic ring

FIGURE 1

6. With someone else holding the ends of the tubes in the pocket, plait them together neatly and evenly to form the tieback. Secure as before by tying with a short length of nylon cord, elastic or cotton thread at the other end. Slip the other pocket over the three tubes at the end, and neatly slip stitch the pocket into position, while tucking under a 1 cm (⅜ in) hem as you stitch.

7. Referring to Step 7 and Figure 1 on page 81, hand stitch a small plastic ring to each end of the tieback so that the top of the plastic ring lies approximately 1 cm (⅜ in) from the outside edge.

8. Repeat Steps 5–7 on this page, plaiting the three remaining tubes to form the second tieback.

VALANCES

A valance not only adds an important finishing touch to your window-dressing, but can also be used to hide exposed rails and unattractive pelmets.

To calculate how much fabric you will need, measure the length of the curtain rail and multiply this measurement by 2 or 2.5 (to allow for gathering). This will be the cutting length of the valance. If you are covering a pelmet, add twice the length of the short side of the pelmet to this measurement. As for curtains, divide the cutting length by the width of the fabric to determine how many drops you need to join.

The finished depth of the valance is normally one fifth of the length of the main curtain. This rule would not apply, however, if you wanted to dress the window with a valance only. In a bathroom, for example, where one might choose not to have curtains, the valance can cover as much as two-thirds of the height of the window.

For more height, mount the rail higher than usual, making sure, though, that this is in keeping with the proportions of the room, and of the window itself. I often suggest this when a valance is to hang over French windows or sliding doors and should not extend too far down into the walk-through of the door.

SHAPED VALANCE
WITH A BORDER

REQUIREMENTS

calico (*see* Steps 1–3, below)
matching cotton thread
contrasting fabric for border
two- or three-cord heading tape

1. Measure the length of the rail and multiply this measurement by 2 or 2.5, depending on how full you would like the valance to be.

2. Decide on the depth of the valance in the centre and at the sides; I usually make the sides no more than 20 cm (8 in) longer than the centre. This is a flexible rule: if, for instance, the window is very wide, a difference of up to 40 cm (15¾ in) is quite acceptable; if the window is narrow, however, I feel 15 cm (6 in) is about the maximum one should allow.

As a general rule, the middle section should cover about half the width of the window, and the long sections about a quarter each.

3. Calculate how many drops you require to achieve the cutting width (remembering that the valance will extend across the full width of the window) by dividing the cutting width (i.e. the width before gathering) by the width of the fabric. Cut the required number of drops for the centre (shortest) section to the desired finished depth plus 5 cm (2 in). Cut the outside drops to the finished depth plus 5 cm (2 in).

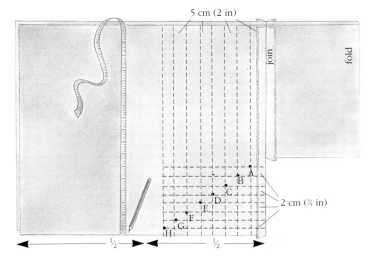

FIGURE 2

4. To join the drops (*see* Figure 1), position one of the long sections right side up and, with right sides together, pin and then stitch the short, centre drop to one side. (If using more than one drop for the centre, join these first.) Open the work, and with right sides together, pin and stitch the other long section to the other edge of the centre section. Overlock or zigzag the raw edges to neaten.

5. With right sides together, fold the valance, halving the centre section. Starting at the point where the centre section joins the side section, and working towards the outside edge, make soft pencil marks at 5 cm (2 in) intervals, each 2 cm (¾ in) closer to the bottom than the previous one, ending about halfway along the bottom edge of the long section (*see* Figure 2). Now join the marks (see points A to H on Figure 2) with a soft line, forming a curve in the process. Cut away the fabric below the line you have drawn.

6. For the border, cut enough strips of contrasting fabric, each 12 cm (4¾ in) wide (or any desired width), to make up the cutting length of the valance when joined. With right sides together, join the strips. With wrong sides together, fold the long strip over, halving its

width. Leaving a 1 cm (⅜ in) seam allowance, pin and straight stitch, forming a tube.

7. With right sides together, and raw edges aligning, stitch the border along the bottom edge of the valance. Overlock or zigzag the raw edges.

8. Working on the wrong side, press the seam allowance towards the valance. On the right side, topstitch about 5 mm (¼ in) from the seamline (*see* Figure 3)

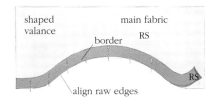

FIGURE 3

9. Turn 2 cm (¾ in) and a then a further 2 cm (¾ in) to the wrong side along both short sides of the valance to form a hem. Blind stitch or straight stitch into position.

10. Working on the wrong side, and measuring from the bottom up, mark the desired finished depth of the valance. If you intend making a little pocket in which to store the cords once the tape has been drawn up, do so at this stage.

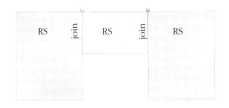

FIGURE 1

(*see* Making a Pocket for the Curtain Cords, page 71). Fold over the excess at the top and position the heading tape 2 cm (¾ in) below the fold, tucking under a short length of tape at the beginning and at the end. Make sure that the raw edge will be hidden by the tape. Stitch the tape to the valance along both edges, and along the two short sides, remembering to hold the cords away from the edge when stitching the side at which the cords will be drawn up.

11. Gather the valance to the desired width. Position a rail on the wall above or in front of the curtain rail, and hang the valance as you would hang a curtain.

HINTS
❀ If the valance is to hang over a pelmet, I suggest that you use two-cord heading tape, allowing a heading of about 3 cm (1¼ in). Leave an opening at each end (i.e. do not stitch the tape down at the sides), so that expanding wire can be threaded through the casing.

❀ If the valance is to hang on a narrow window, use two-cord heading tape.

VARIATIONS
❧ For an extra finishing touch, insert piping between the valance and the border.

❧ Stitch bias binding along the top edge of the heading; this can be co-ordinated with the piping used between the main valance and the border.

❧ A frilled edge also looks good on a straight or shaped valance.

❧ A shaped valance uses quite a lot of fabric, so if you don't have quite enough, consider a simple, straight valance. Make the valance in the same way as the shaped valance, omitting the shaping.

FESTOON BLIND

Festoon blinds are my favourite type of window-dressing as they are really cottagey, but also blend in well with a modern room setting. They are functional and can be used to dress any kind of window, provided the width of the window does not exceed 2.2 m (7 ft) and the length does not exceed 2 m (79 in).

A working festoon blind can be used on its own and does not require a valance or curtains. It can be inserted within the window reveal or can extend beyond it if you wish to create the impression of a larger window.

A point to bear in mind when making a festoon blind is that when the blind is fully raised, it measures about one third of its original length. If you want maximum sunlight when the blind is raised, consider mounting the blind about 30 cm (12 in) above the top of the window reveal. No rail is necessary when installing a festoon blind as it is attached to a wooden batten.

REQUIREMENTS

calico (*see* Steps 1, 2 and 4, below)
matching cotton thread
two- or three-cord heading tape
Velcro
small plastic rings
wooden batten, 2 cm x 2 cm (¾ in x ¾ in) x finished width of blind
screw eyes
2 mm-thick (⅛ in-thick) nylon cord
cleat
toggle

1. Measure the width of the window reveal or, if the blind will extend beyond the reveal, decide on the finished width of the blind. Multiply this figure by 2 to determine the cutting width of the fabric. Divide this figure by the width of the fabric to determine how many drops you require.

2. To calculate the length of the blind, add 20 cm (8 in) to the desired finished length. This extra 20 cm (8 in) allows the blind to balloon at the bottom when the blind is dropped and includes a heading and seam.

3. If necessary, join drops to obtain the desired width (*see* Joining Drops, page 70).

4. Cut the frill twice the cutting width of the blind and about 12 cm (4¾ in) deep (this includes an allowance for the seam and the hem). If necessary, join strips to obtain the required length using French seams (*see* Making a French Seam, page 8). To determine how many strips you need, divide the required length by the width of the fabric. Overlock or zigzag one long side of the frill, and then fold up a hem of 1 cm (⅜ in). Gather the other long side of the frill to fit along the bottom edge of the blind (*see* Gathering a Frill, page 8). With right sides together, pin and stitch into position. On the wrong side, overlock or zigzag the raw edges and press the seam allowance towards the blind. On the right side of the blind, topstitch neatly about 5 mm (¼ in) from the seamline.

5. Turn 1 cm (⅜ in) and then 2.5 cm (1 in) to the wrong side along both sides of the blind; press and blind stitch or straight stitch the hems into position.

6. If you intend making a pocket in which to store the cords once the blind has been gathered, do so at this stage (*see* Making a Pocket for the Curtain Cords, page 71). Fold over a 5 cm (2 in) heading along the top of the blind and pin the heading tape into position 2 cm (¾ in) below the fold, tucking under a short section of tape at the beginning and the end. Make sure that it covers the raw edge of the blind. Straight stitch along the top

and bottom edges of the tape. At the end opposite to that at which you will draw up the cords, stitch down the tucked-under edge of the tape, securing the cords. At the other end, pull a short length of the cords out, tuck under the tape, and stitch the end of the tape down, holding the cords away to avoid catching them in the stitching line.

7. Cut a piece of Velcro as long as the finished width of the blind into three or four equal strips. Working on the wrong side, stitch the strips to the heading tape along their top and bottom edges, taking care not to catch the cords in the stitching, and leaving equal spaces between them. The other side of the Velcro will be stapled or nailed to the wooden batten.

8. Position the blind wrong side up. At the bottom right-hand corner, 5–10 cm (2–4 in) from the side, and 3 cm (1¼ in) above the frill, make a mark with a soft pencil. Repeat on the left-hand side. To determine how many scallops you will have, divide the distance between these two points by 50–75 cm (20–30 in), depending on the width you'd like

Contrast piping has been used on a Festoon Blind to create a luxurious, yet warm and homely feel in this kitchen.

the scallops to be, remembering that the scallops will be halved when the blind has been gathered. The distance between the scallops before gathering should not be less than 50 cm (20 in). (Getting the figures to work may involve having to make adjustments and a certain amount of trial and error.) Once you have decided on the width of the scallops, make soft pencil marks to indicate the position of the vertical lines between the scallops.

9. Starting with the mark 3 cm (1¼ in) from the bottom of the blind (where the frill is attached), and working towards the top of the blind along the lines you have just created, mark points at roughly 25 cm (10 in) intervals. (You may need to adjust these intervals depending on your particular requirements.) Repeat this procedure, working along the other parallel vertical rows you created in Step 8. (The number of rows will depend on the width of the blind.) Hand stitch a plastic ring to the blind at each of the points you have marked (*see* Figure 1).

10. Cut a 2 cm x 2 cm (¾ in x ¾ in) wooden batten to the finished width of the blind and cover the batten with scrap calico. Using a staple gun, panel pins or tiny wood nails, attach a strip of Velcro, cut to the finished width of the blind, to the side of the batten to which the blind will be attached.

11. Gather the blind to the finished width and attach it to the batten, matching up the sections of Velcro.

12. Turn the blind to the wrong side and mark points on the batten that line up with the rings on the blind (*see* Figure 1).

13. Insert screw eyes into the batten at these points. Decide whether you want to operate the blind from the right-hand or the left-hand side, and insert an extra screw eye 1 cm (⅜ in) from the end of the batten on this side. This will hold the weight of all the cords.

14. Lay the blind wrong side up, and, starting at the left-hand side (or the right-hand side if you will be operating the blind from the left), thread 2 mm-thick (⅛ in-thick) nylon cord up through the vertical row of rings (before you cut the cord off the roll, estimate how much you will need by measuring it out). Work the cord up the first vertical row, into the screw eye and then across the width of the blind, passing it through all the screw eyes. Allow a length of cord no more than one third of the length of the blind to hang down the side. Secure the end of the cord at the bottom ring of each vertical row by tying a knot and then burning the ends of the cords to seal them neatly.

15. Once all the cords have been threaded through the last screw eye, tie them together in a knot.

16. Trim the cords to the same length, and plait them together. Thread the ends through a toggle.

17. Detach the top of the blind from the batten, allowing the blind to hang by the cords. Mount the batten on the wall and then attach the blind again using the Velcro.

18. Mount a cleat on the wall about halfway up the blind, making sure that it will be hidden when the blind is dropped. The cleat will hold the excess cord when the blind is raised.

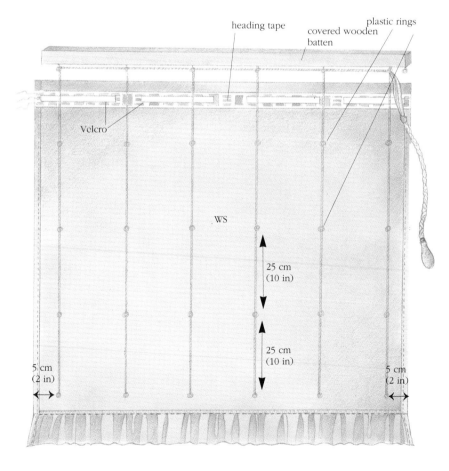

heading tape
covered wooden batten
plastic rings
Velcro
WS
25 cm (10 in)
25 cm (10 in)
5 cm (2 in)
5 cm (2 in)

FIGURE 1

The Mock Festoon Blind in this quite modern setting has been inserted to fit within the window reveal.

VARIATIONS

❦ Attach a frill along the sides of the blind, as well as to the bottom.

❦ For a tailored finish, pleat the frill instead of gathering it.

❦ If you don't like frills, omit them and stitch piping around the edge of the blind instead.

❦ Instead of stitching rings all the way to the top of the blind, stop about halfway up; the result will be a more unusual blind that is puffy only at the bottom.

MOCK FESTOON BLIND

A mock festoon is not a working blind, and is therefore far easier to make than the real thing. Once the vertical rows of tape have been drawn up, the blind cannot be pulled up or down. I usually position the bottom of the blind about halfway or two-thirds of the way down the window.

Mock festoons can be used as a valance in the living room or bedroom, or to dress a window that does not require curtains, such as one made of frosted glass.

REQUIREMENTS

calico (*see* Steps 1–3, below)
matching cotton thread
three-cord heading tape
two-cord heading tape

1. Measure the width of the window reveal, or, if you would like the blind to extend beyond the reveal, decide on the finished width of the blind. Multiply this figure by 2 (to allow for gathering) to determine the cutting width of the fabric. Divide this figure by the width of the fabric to determine the number of drops required.

2. To calculate the cutting length of the blind, multiply the desired finished length of the blind by 2; subtract 10 cm (4 in) from this measurement for the frill. Cut out the fabric to the required measurements.

3. If necessary, join drops to achieve the desired width (*see* Joining Drops, page 70).

4. Multiply the cutting width of the blind by 2 to establish the cutting length of the frill (this allows for gathering). Divide this measurement by the width of the fabric to determine how many strips you will need to make up the frill. Decide on the depth of the frill – I find that 10 cm (4 in)

works well – and add 2 cm (¾ in) to this measurement for the seam allowance and hem before cutting. Join the strips together using French seams (*see* Making a French Seam, page 8). Overlock or zigzag one long edge, then turn back a hem of 1 cm (⅜ in), press and stitch down neatly.

5. Gather the frill (*see* Gathering a Frill, page 8), and with right sides together, pin and then stitch the gathered edge of the frill to the bottom edge of the blind. Overlock or zigzag the raw edges. On the wrong side, press the seam allowance towards the blind; on the right side of the blind, topstitch about 5 mm (¼ in) from the seamline to neaten.

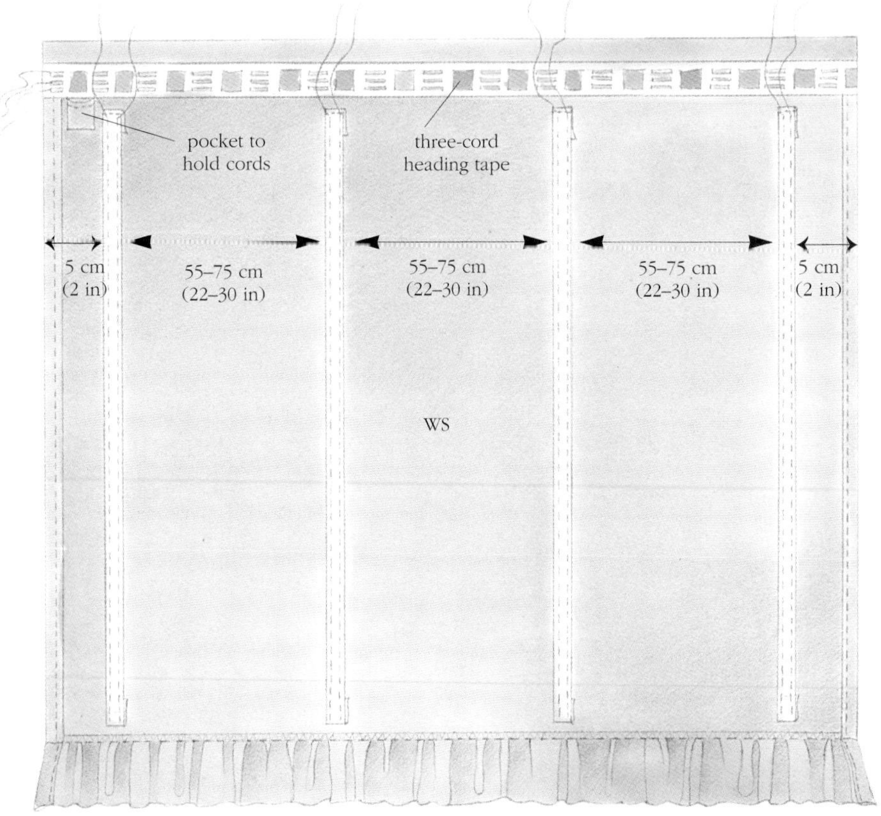

6. Turn 2 cm (¾ in) and then a further 2 cm (¾ in) to the wrong side along both side edges of the blind. Blind stitch or straight stitch the hems into position.

7. If you intend making a little pocket in which to store the cords once the blind has been gathered, do so at this stage (*see* Making a Pocket for the Curtain Cords, page 71). Fold over a 5 cm (2 in) heading at the top of the blind and stitch your three-cord heading tape into position 2–3 cm (¾–1½ in) below the fold. Make sure that the raw edge of the blind is covered by the tape. At the end opposite to that at which you will draw up the cords, stitch down the end of the tape, thus securing the cords. At the other end, pull a short length of the cords out, tuck under a short section of tape, and stitch the end of the tape down, holding the cords away to avoid catching them in the stitching line.

8. Stitch the first vertical row of two-cord heading tape 5 cm (2 in) in from the side hem, tucking under a short section at the top and bottom. Stitch down one side, across the bottom (thus securing the cords at the bottom), and up the other side. At the top, pull out a short length of each of the cords, hold them away from the top of the tape, tuck the end under and stitch down. Repeat on the other side of the blind.

9. Measure the distance between these two rows of tape and divide this figure by a measurement between 55 cm and 75 cm (22 in and 30 in), which will be the distance between the vertical rows of tape (*see* Figure 1). This will give you the number of vertical rows of tape you will need. (Careful calculation, a certain amount of trial and error, and adjustment of measurements may be necessary at this stage.) Mark the positions for the vertical rows of tape on the wrong side of

pocket to hold cords

three-cord heading tape

5 cm (2 in) · 55–75 cm (22–30 in) · 55–75 cm (22–30 in) · 55–75 cm (22–30 in) · 5 cm (2 in)

WS

FIGURE 1

cords tied together to neaten

FIGURE 2

R O M A N   B L I N D

Roman blinds take time to make and require meticulous measuring, marking and stitching, but are a very popular choice of window-dressing because they are not only practical, but give a neat and tailored appearance to the window. They ensure privacy, control light and provide insulation.
A Roman blind looks effective on its own or coupled with mock curtains and a valance. Add a creative touch by inserting a border along all four sides of the blind, attaching a frill along the bottom, or scalloping the edge of the blind.

Do you mount the blind inside or outside the window reveal? Consider an inside mount if you want the woodwork of the window to be seen, or perhaps if you want to keep the window-dressing simple but effective.
If you would like the blind to extend beyond the window reveal, consider mounting it a little distance above the window so that most of the window is exposed when the blind is raised.
Roman blinds are most suitable for a narrow window, but two blinds mounted next to each other can be used to dress a wide window. In this case, be very careful when stitching the blinds and casings so that they line up with each other perfectly.

the blind with a soft pencil, then pin the tape into position and stitch down neatly as before.

10. At the top of the blind, gather up the vertical rows by drawing up the cords, knotting them once you have achieved the desired length. To neaten all the cords hanging down, I link them together by tying the first pair of cords to the second, and so on (*see* Figure 2).

11. Gather the heading tape at the top to the length of the rail, insert your hooks, and hang the blind. DO NOT CUT THE CORDS.

VARIATIONS

❦ Hand-stitch a bow to the blind at the top or bottom of each vertical row.

❦ Attach a continuous frill along both side edges of the blind as well as the bottom. To calculate the total cutting length of your frill, add twice the length of the blind to the width, and double this figure.

❦ Insert piping between the main part of the blind and the frill. Stitch matching bias binding to the edge of the frill to finish.

The creatively scalloped edge of the Roman Blind softens this kitchen.

calico (*see* Steps 1 and 2, below)
matching cotton thread
cotton lining (calico will be more suitable
than polycotton)
Velcro cut to finished width of blind
dowel rods, 3 mm (⅛ in) in diameter
flat wooden batten, 1 cm x 5 cm (⅜ in x 2 in),
10 cm (4 in) shorter than finished width
of blind
small plastic rings
wooden batten, 2 cm x 2 cm (¾ in x ¾ in) x
finished width of blind
screw eyes
2 mm-thick (⅛ in-thick) nylon cord

1. Measure the width of the window reveal, or, if the blind will extend beyond the reveal, decide on the finished width of the blind. To calculate the cutting width and length of your fabric, add 10 cm (4 in) to the desired finished width and 20 cm (8 in) to the desired finished length of the blind.

If the blind is wider than the fabric, you will have to join drops. Divide the width of the blind by the width of the fabric to calculate how many drops you will require, then cut out and join the drops (*see* Joining Drops, page 70). If you wish, decorate the joins with a border, lace, or piping.

2. It will be best to use calico for the lining. The total width required will be the same as for the front of the blind. The length of the lining will depend on how many casings the blind will have – each casing will require 3 cm (1¼ in) of lining. When calculating the cutting length of the lining, I generally add 15–20 cm (6–8 in) to the total cutting length of the blind (*see* Step 1). Any excess can be cut off at a later stage and used for another project.

3. Cut, and if necessary, join, the lining to make up the required size, ensuring that the joins will be in the same places as those on the front of the blind (*see* Joining Drops, page 70). Overlock or

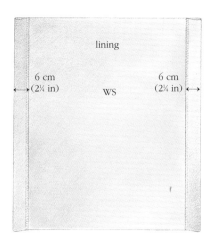

FIGURE 1

zigzag the sides of the lining; then press in a hem of 6 cm (2¼ in) along each side (*see* Figure 1).

4. Lay the lining right side up. Measure 20 cm (8 in) up from the bottom and draw a soft horizontal pencil line in this position all the way across the blind. This will be the stitching line for the first casing. Draw another line parallel to, and 3 cm (1¼ in) above, the

first one. Continue working up the blind, allowing about 25 cm (10 in) between casings (*see* Figure 2). This distance can be adjusted, but bear in mind that the distance between the last casing and the top of the blind should be 1.5 times the distance between the other casings so that the folds will lie neatly on top of one another when the blind is fully raised.

5. With the right side uppermost, fold the lining so that the two pencil lines for the bottom casing meet, and pin. Repeat for each casing. Carefully stitch to form each casing, ensuring that the casings will accommodate the width of the dowel rods you are using.

6. Go back to the bottom edge of the lining and, again working on the right side, draw a soft pencil line 6 cm (2¼ in) below the stitch line for the bottom casing (*see* Figure 3). This will eventually form the casing for the flat wooden batten, which you will insert in Step 15. Set the lining aside.

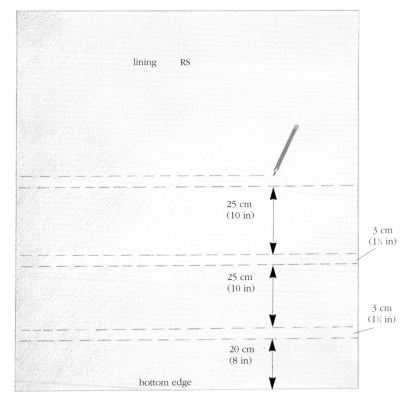

FIGURE 2

92

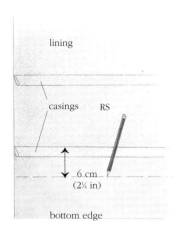

FIGURE 3

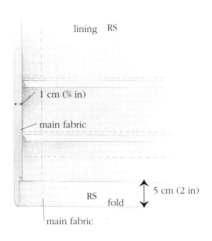

FIGURE 4

7. Overlock or zigzag the raw edges down the sides of the front of the blind. Press 5 cm (2 in) to the wrong side.

8. With right sides together, raw edges at the bottom aligned, and leaving a 2 cm (¾ in) seam allowance, stitch the lining to the main fabric along the bottom edge, bearing in mind that the lining will be slightly narrower. Trim the seam down to 1 cm (⅜ in) and overlock or zigzag the raw edges.

9. Turn the blind right side out, and with the lining uppermost, fold up 5 cm (2 in) along the bottom edge so that the main fabric extends 5 cm (2 in) onto the lining side of the blind (*see* Figure 4 at the top of the next column).

10. Lay the blind flat, lining uppermost, and smooth out both layers. Working from the bottom to the top, tack the front of the blind and the lining together in a line about 10 cm (4 in) from each of the side edges (*see* Figure 5) so that the two layers stay together.

11. Stitch the lining and the front of the blind together right across the width of the blind, just above the stitching line for each casing. Fold each casing towards the bottom of the blind and work

carefully and neatly, ensuring that you don't catch the casing in the stitching (*see* Figure 5). Working along the line drawn on the lining 6 cm (2¼ in) below the bottom casing, stitch the lining to the blind to form the batten casing.

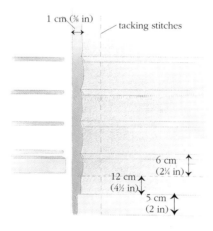

FIGURE 5

12. Working on the lining side of the blind, and measuring from the bottom edge upwards, carefully mark off the finished length of the blind, plus 2 cm (¾ in) along the top. Cut off any excess fabric (from both layers, if necessary) along the top of the blind. Fold the extra 2 cm (¾ in) that you allowed towards the back of the blind and press neatly.

13. Working on the lining side, stitch down a strip of Velcro (cut to the width of the finished blind) 5 mm (¼ in) below the top fold, making sure that the raw edge of the heading is covered by the Velcro (*see* Figure 6). Remove the tacking stitches you made in Step 10.

14. With a small French knot, hand stitch the lining to the blind at the mid-point between casings (*see* Figure 6).

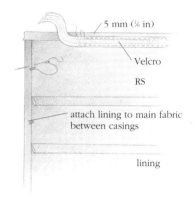

FIGURE 6

15. Cut the dowel rods to the correct length and insert into the casings. Insert the flat wooden batten into its casing at the bottom of the blind.

16. Hand stitch the plastic rings to the folded edges of the casings. The outer two rings should be 5 cm (2 in) from the edges of the lining. The distance between vertical rows of rings should be

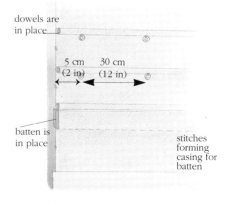

FIGURE 7

about 30 cm (12 in) – I usually measure the distance between the two outer rings and divide this measurement by 30 (12) to establish how many rows of rings I need. Using this as a guide, decide on the distance between rows.

17. Cover the 2 cm x 2 cm (¾ in x ¾ in) wooden batten with scrap calico. Attach the relevant strip of Velcro to the batten using a staple gun or small wood nails.

18. Attach the blind to the batten, matching up the Velcro strips. Mark the positions of the screw eyes on the underside of the batten, exactly in line with the plastic rings on the blind, and screw in. Screw in one extra screw eye about 1 cm (⅜ in) from the end of the batten on the side from which you will operate the blind.

19. Starting on the side opposite to where you want the draw cord to be, tie one end of the nylon cord to the bottom plastic ring, thread the cord up through each ring and through the screw eyes along the top, allowing the loose end of the cord to hang about a third of the way down the length of the blind. Repeat until each vertical row of rings has been threaded.

20. Knot the cords together at the point where they come through the extra screw eye. Trim the cords to the same length, plait and thread the ends through a toggle.

21. Detach the blind from the wooden batten so that it hangs by the cords, and mount the batten in position on the wall, or within the window reveal, using a screw at each end and one in the middle to add extra support if necessary.

22. Mount a cleat on the wall about halfway up the blind, making sure that it will be hidden by the blind. The cleat holds the excess cord when the blind is raised.

BOX-PLEATED FESTOON BLIND

A box-pleated festoon blind is tailored at the top, yet soft and feminine at the bottom. It is made up of deep inverted pleats that fall into puffs that scallop at the bottom. No frill is attached to this blind, but piping stitched around all four sides adds a nice finishing touch. You can also decorate the top of the blind with fabric bows.

REQUIREMENTS

calico (*see* Steps 1 and 2, below)
matching cotton thread
polycotton for lining (optional)
piping (optional)
Velcro cut to finished width of blind
small plastic rings
wooden batten, 2 cm x 2 cm (¾ in x ¾ in) x
finished width of blind
screw eyes
2 mm-thick (⅛ in-thick) nylon cord
cleat

1. Measure the width of the window reveal, or, if the blind will extend beyond the reveal, decide on the finished width of the blind.

2. Before you cut the fabric, calculate how many pleats the blind will have, remembering that the size of the pleats will determine the fullness of the puffs at the bottom of the blind. I usually make the pleats about 15 cm (6 in) deep (therefore allowing 30 cm [12 in] per pleat), and about 30–45 cm (12–18 in) apart (*see* Figure 1), but this will depend on the width of your window. Multiply the number of pleats by the full allowance for each pleat; add this figure to the desired finished width of the blind to determine the cutting width of the fabric. To determine the cutting length of the fabric, add 30 cm (12 in) to the finished length of the blind to allow for fullness.

3. If you would like to attach piping to the edges of the blind, it is a good idea to use a lining, as this will hide the raw edges of the piping. Cut the lining to the same size as the main fabric.

4. If desired, stitch piping all around the blind on the right side of the main fabric, with the rounded edge of the piping lying

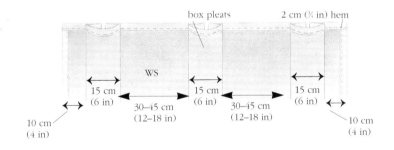

FIGURE 1

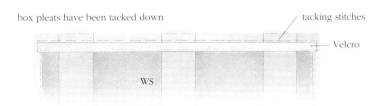

FIGURE 2

A softly tailored Box-pleated Festoon Blind is suited to this romantic setting.

(12–18 in) (*see* Figure 1). To create a pleasing overall effect, it is very important to position the pleats with equal distances between them – getting this right will take careful planning and calculating, and may involve some trial and error.

6. Working on the wrong side, securely tack each pleat down flat close to the top of the blind (*see* Figure 2). Position and pin a strip of Velcro 1 cm (⅜ in) from the top, then stitch along all four edges of the Velcro to attach, securing the pleats in the process (*see* Figure 2). Remove all the tacking stitches.

7. On the wrong side, hand stitch a vertical row of plastic rings to the centre of each pleat (*see* Figure 3). The first ring should be about 10 cm (4 in) from the bottom of the blind and the distance between rings should be approximately 25–30 cm (10–12 in).

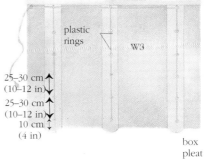

plastic rings

W3

25–30 cm (10–12 in)

25–30 cm (10–12 in)

10 cm (4 in)

box pleat

FIGURE 3

8. Complete the blind by covering the wooden batten, attaching the screw eyes in the appropriate places, inserting the nylon cord, and so on, following Steps 17–22 for the Roman Blind on page 94.

HINT
❋ If the window is very narrow, consider making the blind with only two pleats, positioned 15 cm (6 in) from the sides of the blind. The result will be a blind with a single soft scallop.

towards the centre of the blind. With right sides together, attach the lining to the blind, leaving an opening of 15–20 cm (6–8 in) along one side. Turn the work right side out. If you have not used lining, turn a 2 cm (¾ in) hem to the wrong side along the sides, the top (*see* Figure 1) and bottom.

5. With the lining or the wrong side of the blind uppermost, and starting about 10 cm (4 in) from the top left-hand edge of the blind, carefully pin the first inverted pleat into position (*see* Figure 1). You can also tack it down if you wish. Remember that the distance between pleats should be 30–45 cm

INDEX